HEALTHWAYS

Newfoundland elders:
their lifestyles and values

R.R. Andersen, J.K. Crellin & B. O'Dwyer

HEALTHWAYS

Newfoundland elders:
their lifestyles and values

R.R. Andersen, J.K. Crellin & B. O'Dwyer

Creative Publishers
St. John's, Newfoundland
1998

THE CANADA COUNCIL | LE CONSEIL DES ARTS
FOR THE ARTS | DU CANADA
SINCE 1957 | DEPUIS 1957

We acknowledge the support of the Canada Council for the Arts for our publishing program.

Cover and Illustrations: Sylvia Ficken ©1998

∝ Printed on acid-free paper

Published by
CREATIVE BOOK PUBLISHING
a division of 10366 Newfoundland Limited
a Robinson-Blackmore Printing & Publishing associated company
P.O. Box 8660, St. John's, Newfoundland A1B 3T7

Printed in Canada by:
ROBINSON-BLACKMORE PRINTING & PUBLISHING

Canadian Cataloguing in Publication Data

Andersen, Raoul, 1936–

Healthways

Includes bibliographical references and index.
ISBN 1-895387-97-3

1. Aged — Newfoundland.
2. Medical anthropology — Newfoundland.
3. Newfoundland — Social life and customs.
4. Medical care — Newfoundland — History.
I. Crellin, J.K. II. O'Dwyer, Bernard. III. Title.

R463.N44A6 1998   305.26'09718   C98-950150-7

Contents

PREFACE

*T*his volume began as an exploration of changing health care beliefs and practices in Newfoundland during the first half of the twentieth century. We sought to capture the changes through the voices of those who participated in them. One reason for the exploration was to look at not only the dramatic impact of changes in health care, but also in Newfoundland lifestyles. Our thought was that because of the changes Newfoundland's older and younger generations may well have very different values and understandings about living healthy lives.

We believe that the results of this exploration, albeit based mainly upon listening to the older generation, confirm this expectation. Moreover, much understanding is provided about the place of values amid times of change and stress. The voices of the elders, too, offer wonderfully fresh images of the challenges of life in Newfoundland, challenges that resonate with rural life elsewhere.

The voices are printed verbatim with silent editing to smooth reading. While we have changed the names of informants, most names mentioned by informants are as given.

We have acquired many debts during the exploration. Our greatest is to the many seniors who, in typical Newfoundland fashion, generously opened their doors to interviewers and shared their memories and ideas. We have tried to do justice to all that they told and taught us. They wanted to pass their wisdom on. We hope that the opportunity to share their memories and feelings with us was of help to them.

Research for this study was supported by a grant from the Institute for Social and Economic Research (ISER), Memorial University of Newfoundland. We also wish to acknowledge the participation of our colleague, Dr. Michael Murray, who was part of this project during its data gathering stage.

Thanks are due to ISER's Janet Oliver for most helpfully managing our project affairs. Discussions with informants were conducted during the summer 1992 by Gillian Tooton and Romaine Whelan. We express our gratitude to them for their strong commitment and contributions to this project. We thank also our transcribers, Laura Taylor and Angela White, for many hours devoted to producing transcriptions of tape recordings that are the primary data for this volume. We are especially grateful to Angela White for her patient revision and production of the many drafts that had to be made before we had our ideas "about right."

Our interviewing contacts on the Avalon Peninsula were eased most graciously by Mrs. Mary Luther, The Retired Citizens' Centre, Sister Patricia Marie, McAuley Convent, Mrs. Judy Quigley, St. Patrick's Mercy Home, and Mrs. Judy Cook, Seniors Outreach Project.

Lastly, we are very grateful for the eagle eye of Carmelita McGrath who gave us innumerable, valuable editorial suggestions.

I *Listening and understanding*

The people who come to see us [doctors] bring us their stories. They hope they tell them well enough so that we understand the truth of their lives. They hope we know how to interpret their stories correctly. (Robert Coles, *The Call of Stories*, 1989)

Healthways is about people, their time and place, their health and ill-health, and the values that sustained them in their earlier and later years. From the voices of these elderly people we learn about their lifestyle, attitudes, beliefs and values. They recall these from early childhood, through their working days, to their retirement and up to the present.

Robert Coles, from whom we take the opening quotation, believes doctors and other health care professionals have a special responsibility to elicit and listen to such stories, to understand the complex relationships between health and social circumstances. However, as Coles observes, interpreting these stories is difficult.

We have three purposes in presenting these recollections. One is to listen to elders, to let them speak for themselves, for they have fascinating stories to tell. Secondly, we focus attention on one broad issue relevant within and beyond Newfoundland: To what extent do individual values associated with lifestyles influence the maintenance of health and the treatment of illness? And, further, does an apprecia-

1

tion of these values help us to understand how many elders cope with their changing identity as senior citizens? Our third purpose is to comment on the place of values in society today. We need to ask about the significance of values in health care for everyone concerned with our health care system, the general public, health care practitioners and policy makers.

We have relied heavily on extensive quotes from our informants for several reasons. Increasingly, scholars have shown that narratives offer an invaluable way to uncover the beliefs in people's lives, the ambiguities, the uncertainties, the perceptions of communities and the way they relate them to the immediate world around themselves. Often one sees in narratives efforts to make both the past and present more comprehensible, if not compatible—a way to make sense of one's life. Questionnaires have their place in finding information, but like statistics, they reveal people with "the tears wiped off."

We must also make clear what the study is not. We did not set out to isolate and evaluate, using questionnaires and control groups, the significance of particular traits in coping with age and illness. Our interest in values emerged from our interpretation of the informants' accounts of their upbringing, their work, their attitudes to maintaining health, and how they handled illnesses. In other words we identified what the informants themselves see as *their* values. As we elaborate later, we see these values not so much as the universal moral kind, but as individual guidelines—secular or based on religious teachings—that our informants saw as necessary for the well-being of their family and community. Individuals and groups often speak of their values, such as family, honesty, a good living and so on, and we wondered about the roster of concerns, factors or "values" that ordered the lives of the elderly Newfoundlanders that we met.

We chose not to ask direct questions on such matters, since they may have overly shaped informants' answers. This accounts for the lack of comments on various dispositions and habits (e.g. optimism, smoking, drinking) commonly considered in models of coping developed by social scientists. We are not saying these are irrelevant to our informants' ways of coping, but we took the approach of trying to uncover what our informants themselves identified. Understanding this can be invaluable in many situations when friends, relatives, counsellors, or health professionals need to offer help and advice.

We read informants' accounts and responses to questions for both individual and collective life experiences. These voices reveal individual identities rooted in Newfoundland. They emerge from innumerable interactions between personalities and the environment, and from the unshaped and ambiguous experiences begun at birth, through maturation and adulthood, and into old age. At the same time, the narratives collectively offer more than individual identities. They reveal continuities in experiences, attitudes and understandings widely met within Newfoundland. By listening to the combination of individual voices, we learn about group identities and about social pressures encouraging self-discipline through, for example, the power of the clergy.

Informants were raised generally in small, often remote and necessarily self-sufficient outports where no one was a stranger, and one relied first upon family, friends and neighbours for most health needs. In their senior years the informants reflect, measure and judge their situations. They allow for considerations of where they stand in the present in relationship to the younger generations that are responsible for the future in a society increasingly urban, secular, mobile, cash-market driven and state-dominated. Implicitly or explicitly, their observations ask: Are my hopes, ideas and beliefs valid and relevant? Has the new generation heeded my example, instructions and lessons? Where do I fit in this present world?

The last question expresses the search for meaning. Informants' responses are mixed, sometimes comforting, often uncertain. This is no surprise. In industrial societies like our own, change is more typical and expected than are tradition and continuity, and differences between generations is much greater. By contrast, although this risks oversimplification, the comparison between generations was (and is) less sharp in smaller, ethnically homogeneous, nonindustrial, and, socially, largely unstratified communities as found in Newfoundland. What we find in Newfoundland is also one expression of Euro-North American small or rural community life in the first half of the twentieth century. Our data are derived from lives shaped largely by fishing and other maritime activities. Life in small maritime communities had (and still has) much in common with the rural experience everywhere. They share relative isolation and a sense of political marginality from urban-industrial centres with their concentration of social and medical resources. In such rural settings, life was greatly shaped by local resources where families divided their labour between market and subsistence production. Formal schooling was limited (the one room school was typical), and the church was the spiritual and social centre of family and community life. Strong pressures favoured self-discipline, self-sufficiency, and reliance upon and confidence in established ways. Resigned acceptance guided much daily conduct.

Chapter II, primarily through four individual narratives, details many aspects of Newfoundland life from around 1900 to 1950; at the same time, we see the values associated with Newfoundland lifestyles. The next two chapters, largely through short excerpts, look at specific experiences that we suggest have a bearing on maintaining health and coping with illness. The final two chapters look at their present situation in the context of our informants' past lives and their views of today. We suggest that values associated with past lifestyles endure to help many elderly Newfoundlanders cope with their own aging, infirmities, and changing place in society.

●

Informants for this study were selected through random networking. The interviewers found that elders preferred personal contact before consenting to an interview. Therefore, interviewees were asked if they knew of another elder in another community who might consent to an interview. When a person was named, the interviewer and frequently the elder would call the next informant and seek permission for an interview. Through this process we were able to cover a good cross section of the province, by age (over sixty), gender, occupation, geography and religion.

We interviewed a full generation of elders, ranging from sixty-two to ninety-two years old. There were seventeen females and thirteen males. Of these, three women had never married, two were sisters in a religious convent; all the men were married. Our informants covered many occupations from the trades to the professions.

Many communities in Newfoundland were settled by culture and religion. The southern shore, which extends from Petty Harbour to the east side of Placentia Bay, was settled largely by Irish Catholics and their descendants who hold their culture dear. Their ethnic homogeneity and small population have kept their southern shore dialect distinctive and their religious identification strong. By contrast, the northern shore, which ranges from Pouch Cove to approximately Carbonear in Conception Bay, was settled by a mixture of English, Scottish, and Irish. It had a considerably larger population which was pocketed by diverse cultural and religious groups. During the lives of our informants one of the towns on this shore, Harbour Grace, was a major trade centre and competitive with the capital, St. John's. This small urban centre was divided by Carter's Hill into the west end and the east end. The former area had a mixed cultural and religious population; the latter was more populated and had larger pockets of Irish Catholics.

Ten Irish Catholic informants came from communities along the southern shore; three Anglicans, four Catholics and one United Church informant came from communities along the northern shore; and four Anglicans, four Catholics, and one United Church informant came from St. John's. Of the other informants, two were Catholics from the Codroy Valley (western Newfoundland) and Bonavista Bay respectively; two were United Church from southern Labrador.

St. John's and the outports, especially those nearby, have a long history of close social relationships built upon trade, employment, and migration to the city. Few St. John's families lack outport relationships of some kind, and people living in the two settings have much in common. This was evident among those of our informants now residing in St. John's who indicated continuing close ties with their outport home communities.

Semi-structured, tape-recorded interviews were conducted with each individual over two visits. Discussions with informants sought to cover all aspects of health and illness, including major and minor diseases and injuries. Questions were purposely general and open-ended, to allow a free exchange and to elicit whatever informants might recollect and think about. At times, questions were clumsily put as happens in long, informal interviewing sessions. Occasionally, the interviewer phrased a question in a way that steered the informant to a particular conclusion; however, where this was observed we excluded the responses.

Our data have other limitations. Tape-recorded interviews administered by strangers do place those interviewed on stage where they might be prompted to deliver recollections that would not be chosen in other circumstances. We hope this has been minimized by interviewing in the person's own surroundings and by careful choice of two interviewers who were mature women, patient and knowledgeable. Although thirty in-depth structured interviews are a sufficient number for this study—an exploration of health experience, attitudes and values among a population subgroup—we developed our comments with consideration of other literature about Newfoundland (see the Recommended Reading section at the end of this volume.)

For the most part, editing of the carefully transcribed voices has been minimal aside from removing questions, prompts, and repetitions. Reasons why the narratives often flow so well relate, in large part, to rich memories kept alive by large families, once commonplace in Newfoundland. "I have eleven children myself, an adopted one, and foster children. I had twenty-four altogether." Our informants lived very busy lives. Often events told to us had obviously been related many times before to families and friends. This prompted not only sharp recollections of growing up, of school, going to church, helping parents with countless chores, but also memories of illness, especially of childhood illnesses. Scarlet fever, tuberculosis and less serious conditions have left strong impressions, as did changed social circumstances. The latter were sometimes occasioned by a personal illness, or the need to leave school, perhaps to care for a mother or other family members.

Although our informants often described home remedies of the past in specific, practical detail and with a sense of familiarity "Do this," "take that"—we have given little of this recipe information here. Much of it is available elsewhere. Instead, we have focused attention on experiences of and attitudes to health and managing illness.

Special comment is necessary about the accuracy of the memories of the informants. Anthropologists and other social scientists have long been concerned over informants' accuracy. This is particularly true when recalling specific events, as well as selective use of choice stories to support perceptions of the ideal self. Various studies indicate considerable discrepancies between memory and data recorded at the time of an event, for example, a mother's recall of a child's behaviour. There are concerns, too, over tendencies to underestimate, to telescope time; events in the past are often recalled as more recent than they actually are. We believe that inaccuracies and inconsistencies, if they exist, are not significant for the way we use the narratives.

Having said that, the seemingly rosy picture of the past needs questioning. "It was all singing and dancing then, and, to tell you the truth, there wasn't much disease on the go." Readers should wonder why the narratives do not reflect more of the bleak history of Newfoundland in the first half of the century. This was a time of economic disruption and disadvantages for this generation. We have to ask whether or not many have forgotten, or choose to push to one side, hard times and isolation. It is often stated that memories are commonly organized and presented for effect. Certainly, we sense a defensiveness about the old days and against the many negative views that have been expressed about New-foundland life in the past and present. This is linked with pride in self-reliance and survival, which we consider later: "You grew up; you accepted it all; you weren't looking for anything better. And you weren't turning to the government for anything."

As editors, we have faced a dilemma in deciding on the best way to present the often evocative memories, along with our own less colourful commentary. We recognize that analysis and narrative with their strongly contrasting styles are uneasy bedfellows. We can only hope we have not intruded too much on the voices of our informants.

II "The way it was:" lifestyles

The extensive narratives in this chapter offer "bird's-eye" views of Newfoundland life during the earlier part of this century. As we listen to these Newfoundland elders, it becomes clear that they had to cope constantly with everyday hardships, as well as health problems. This was certainly true up to the 1950s and for many even up to the present. We suggest that the circumstances of Newfoundland life fostered such values as self-sufficiency, resourcefulness, pragmatism; prudence, an acceptance of what life has to offer, an appreciation of order and personal discipline, of belonging, fitting in and knowing one's place in history.

We consider these values emerged not only from family life, but also from the way children were brought up, the nature of their schooling and the strong role of churches. These values were also reinforced by the multitude of subsistence and other activities undertaken by those working in the fishery. Indeed, the whole rather diverse and demanding pattern of Newfoundland life was relevant to their values.

Moreover, it is in the stories of our informants' lives that one sees the shaping of attitudes toward gender issues and the power structure within communities. Above all, in this chapter we get a sense of belonging to what some call a "people's world." The narratives raise questions about relationships between values and behaviour, looking after one's health, coping with illnesses and old age, as well as implica-

9

tions for the health care system today. We pursue all of these with some detail in later chapters.

The Newfoundland context

Our informants grew up prior to mid-century, when health care in Newfoundland was undergoing change and scrutiny. St. John's was benefiting from the growth of medical institutions already established. The three key hospitals were: The General, The Grace, and St. Clare's Mercy hospital. As well, there was a hospital for mental and nervous diseases, locally known as the "Mental." Cottage hospitals were also making an impact in rural Newfoundland, as did district nurses and NONIA (the Newfoundland Outport Nursing and Industrial Association). Increasing government involvement in Newfoundland health care took many directions. Two issues in particular received much official attention: tuberculosis and nutrition. The Commission Government (1932-1949), charged with running Newfoundland after the island's bankruptcy, along with a core of reform-minded individuals, ensured that medical developments reached most parts of the island and Labrador. In 1949, Confederation with Canada brought new financial and institutional resources to expand professional health care services across the Province of Newfoundland.

Along with these new resources, the 1950s were a time of general optimism about medicine. A continual stream of advances was being reported, ranging from kidney transplants to many new "wonder" drugs. Public health officials spoke enthusiastically about a wide range of improvements. As conventional medical care became more accessible, lay practitioners, once commonplace, and many longstanding home-treatments were generally pushed aside.

Bounty and dissolution

Changes in health care services were only one facet of broad changes that occurred throughout Newfoundland's coastal society from the 1920s onwards. These changes had far-reaching implications for the lifestyles of Newfoundlanders.

Industrialism, wage labour and the cash economy came rather late to Newfoundland. It began only shortly before the turn of the century, with the establishment of rail, forest industries and pulpwood production, and mining. These developments challenged the centuries-old, labour intensive, manual harvest of marine and land resources. By the late 1940s onwards, industrialization in Newfoundland's fishing industry meant big capital ownership of fleets of large mechanized groundfish trawlers and fish processing plants. These became the economic backbone of major "fish plant towns" or, as government called them, "growth centres," and opportunities for full-time wage labour and technical crafts. Outport people were encouraged (some say "forced") to resettle to these towns where they provided labour for the new fishing industry. Such centralization also improved access to educational, health, and other social services. Many lives and communities were radically changed by these developments. Whether this meant real improvement in family and individual well-being remains a long-running debate. Many informants decried the decline of self-sufficiency and loss of their homes and communities.

In recent years, changes in mechanization, shipping, highway development and transportation, and other factors have greatly reduced or eliminated employment in the industrial sectors. For example, the Newfoundland railway is gone and only a handful of boats remain in the coastal shipping fleet. In 1992, evidence of historically unparalleled stock decline led the federal government to impose a moratorium on the Newfoundland fishing industry's key resource, the northern cod stock. Soon after, moratoria were placed on several other stocks. The first moratorium may continue until the end of the century, even longer.

The moratorium's most immediate human consequences have been lost employment for thirty thousand or more fishers and other industry workers. This was followed by family instability, elderly displacements and long-term uncertainty. The moratorium's effects have aggravated the burden of Canada's highest provincial unemployment rates, endured for more than two decades. And it has renewed old suspicions of a continuing secret government agenda to resettle Newfoundland's outports. These developments underline the wisdom of being suspicious of government, scientific, and other authorities, and their "expert" forecasting and posturing.

Culturally, small fishing communities and Newfoundland once meant one and the same thing. Today, the way Newfoundlanders think about the sea and its resources, and the fishing industry and labour force they sustain, are all in the process of destruction and reconstruction. The province now has a net population loss, and the future of many outport communities is in serious doubt. Although offshore oil and recent mineral finds are promising, continuing uncertainties remain part of Newfoundland's way of life, just as is coping with them.

Church and community

We hear a great deal nowadays about the "healthy community" with questions about whether Newfoundland communities are changing. Belief in a healthy community goes beyond public health issues to a consideration of personal relationships and of levels of communication within a community itself. It is commonplace to say that Newfoundland outports were neighbourly. The kitchen door was always open as a sign of neighbourliness, and the outport kitchen was the centre of community social relationships. "No one is a stranger" was a common enough expression on the island.

Amidst this often challenging environment, which encouraged an appreciation of the need to share even amongst personal animosities, the church became the spiritual and social centre of Newfoundland communities. Among our informants, however, there was a contrast in the memories related to the general geographic area in which they lived. Those from the Catholic southern shore generally remember their early lives as happy times when family members worked together despite the hardships of life. The fishery and their household gardens were provident. Although the work was hard, it was a time when families worked together, played together and prayed together. Garden parties and religious feast days, especially Christmas, were days of excitement and holidaying when the whole community responded to the occasion.

In contrast, our informants from the northern shore, predominantly Protestant, did not recall their early lives with the same enthusiasm. They expressed a sense of difficult times with very little employment. The riches of the fishery and gardens did not receive the same attention. Although this may have had as much to do with geography as religion, church related events are not always remembered as a joyful part of the community's activities. Christmas was perhaps the only time when one got little more than an apple and a few candies "because people were so poor." While two major authority figures existed within most communities — the priest/clergyman and the merchant — the priest generally had a more authoritative presence in shaping everyday relationships.

The church shaped individual lives in many specific ways. "The church controlled your life then more or less. It was all built around the church." Those who remembered singing hymns "around the table every Sunday evening with our hymn book," after spending much of the day at church, spoke for many. "We had to be at church in the morning and Sunday school in the afternoon and church in the night." Some informants remembered "You might get a stick when you came home if you missed it."

Beyond attending church on Sunday, the day itself was considered sacred in other ways. "For each Sunday you had to clean on Saturday, get a shave and a wash and peel all the potatoes and turnip and cabbage." And, "Oh, yes, Sunday, we couldn't even slide on Sunday. We couldn't even get out in our swings, we weren't allowed to swing, we weren't allowed to pick berries." This discipline was, perhaps, more true of Protestant than Catholic communities. Memories of disciplined Sundays often extended to sharing time or food with family and neighbours, a reminder that "basically, neighbour helped neighbour."

School

Although informants had mixed recollections of school—usually a one-room school—the way it instilled a sense of discipline and of order remains sharp in their memories. "My grandmother had the real remedy for staying home from school. If you stayed home she'd put on the castor oil or senna leaves and if you took that you spent your day in the outhouse"; "Going to school, if you did anything wrong, the teacher slapped you. That was the custom"; and, "often you were kept in; there was no activities. You had to stay in school then if you didn't know your lessons. As we said, you had to stay in till maybe four-thirty or five until you learnt them."

A sense of struggling together to seek an education was also felt and perhaps contributed to a sense of order: "We went to school as long as we could." Only a few of our informants finished senior associate or grade eleven. Many reasons were given. An illness or death of a mother with a large family necessitated the removal of a child from school. "I don't have good memories of it. I had to leave and take care of the rest of the family." Maybe, too, personal illness intervened: "I finished school at thirteen. I went to the sanatorium, I realized that I was an ignoramus and I began to read, and I picked up a bit of education." The need for an extra hand on the flakes or in the dory interrupted or ended a young boy's schooling, beginning a different kind of education. "I went to school in the water! I was fishing in the bow of a dory when I was fourteen years of age."

Schools encouraged self-reliance: "We used to bring a junk of wood every morning." "You weren't driven to school either. You walked out with your big wool stockings on you in the winter and your bit of lunch." There were also chores to be done before school and after; informants made it clear there was little time for play. "We had vegetables to set, a potato garden to set; we had to dig those potatoes in the fall and we had hay to cut and make it, and put it in, because we kept a horse and a cow for milk. That had to be done in the fall, so you didn't need games and things like that because you had all kinds of exercise." And there was the fishery: "We used to have to make up the fish on the beach, cure the fish for the winter, you know, salt fish. That's the only way they used to sell their fish years ago, was salt fish. We wouldn't get out of school until three-thirty. Then, in the fall of the year, that'd be late. So we'd have to go then and help the men do the fish and the hay."

Pressures to stay in school varied. "My grandparents, they had nothing and they wanted you to have it. I had to keep going to school." Gender differences were another factor. "Mostly the girls got all the education and the boys got all the work. All my sisters went as high as they could go." This was especially so for those living in St. John's. "I had one sister; she went to Littledale School. The only sister we had and mother said, "Well, we only had one girl so she could afford to send her to Littledale." Gender matters were expressed in other ways. "Before I came along, we had male teachers teaching the boys, and we had a priest, then they brought in the nuns, and there was no mercy in them. No, they were selfish individuals."

The family

Religious, educational and other factors did much to shape a sense of order and self-sufficiency, and other values, yet individual families varied in their fortunes. Some suffered materially and health-wise from losing a family member; perhaps a mother died in child birth or a father perished prematurely as many did when fishing. Young children were often left to be raised by grandparents, and older siblings to be adopted by cousins, or to become wards of the state. In these and other circumstances children faced strong pressures to contribute support to their families.

Some households enjoyed advantages, by virtue of a wife's management skills and a husband's success at fishing or another occupation. Many communities had established merchant families engaged in fish and other aspects of trade, and vessel ownership. Their material, lifestyle and power advantages were quite perceptible. It is fair to speak of some families, like the fish merchant families of Grand Bank and Harbour Breton on the south coast, as *parvenu aristocrats*. In the provincial capital, St. John's, the class distinction was considerable.

Individuals and families often felt badly done by their circumstances, and many saw the merchants as exploitive in their dealings with the fishers and other families. Financial returns from fishing were often meagre, and always uncertain, and generations of Newfoundlanders left their homes in search of better economic opportunities elsewhere. For those who remained, their hardships and the sense of exploitation were tempered by the fact that most in their small, homogeneous and largely egalitarian communities faced the same problems.

The division of labour in fishing households was largely gender based, but it was also pragmatic. Men and women alike pitched in where help was needed. Men were generally responsible for physically heavy and dangerous work—especially going to sea, while women cared for family and home. Boys learned early to help at fishing and other "male" tasks outside the household. Fathers and sons worked together at inshore or offshore fishing and other marine enterprises. As well, they prepared the main garden for planting, and harvested wood and game from surrounding forests and barrens. Some men became seasonal migrant workers; many contracted to harvest pulpwood for the paper industry. Most men went into the forest near their homes each fall to cut wood for home heating, and construction of homes, boats, flakes, and other structures. Boys also sometimes helped with household, cooking, garden chores, and the care of their animals.

Most outport women married, and as wives, mothers, and managers of households they became directly or indirectly involved in the fishing industry. Many Newfoundlanders remember the life of the fisher's wife as completely intertwined with that of her husband. However, formal education allowed some women to enter employment as clerks or secretaries with local merchants and others became teachers and nurses. On the other hand, because of more difficult circumstances, many became domestics, "in service" to other families, even if only for a short time.

From an early age, girls learned how to cook, sew, knit, and clean. They also assisted in the care of animals, gardening and other subsistence production activities. Mothers and daughters also helped with preparing and mending fishing gear—often in the kitchen. Large families often found their responsibilities especially heavy when their men went away to sea and other work. In the offshore and inshore sectors, women worked at fish processing. Some sailed to the Labrador coast each summer, where they cooked and assisted fishing crews operating from shore premises.

Employment opportunities with firms and institutions in St. John's, of course, were more varied. The city was an employment magnet for individuals and families from fishing outports. Men found work as labourers, craftsmen, and clerks in wholesale and retail establishments. Others worked with firms associated with coastal shipping and vessel maintenance, the Newfoundland Dockyard, and the Railway. Some became small entrepreneurs. Many women found clerical work or domestic service with the city's many wealthy families.

Through the mid-twentieth century, the organization of family, work, and religious life in Newfoundland communities fostered a strong disposition toward self-discipline, self-reliance and adaptability. Individuals learned roles and values that stressed hard work undertaken without complaint, and personal and technical skills that served resourcefulness and coping. Ill fortune often visited, and government social "safety nets" were modest or nonexistent. So it was common to share what one had with family members, and, when need be, with neighbours.

Having said this, how did individuals actually see themselves? How did they learn to cope? The following narratives not only illustrate many of our comments, but also help us to understand that such questions permit neither singular nor simple answers.

Listening to Newfoundland Voices

Sister Catherine Daly, b. 1899, Placentia Bay

Our first extended narrative is from a religious sister born into a large family of Irish Catholic descent. She was the first of three children of a tri-part family. Both her parents had been previously married, but their spouses had died. She grew up in an isolated community of Red Island, Placentia Bay, one of many fishing communities on Newfoundland's southern coastline. Generations before, fisher families settled these islands to be near the plentiful fishing grounds. There, they forged a way of life that reflected strong discipline and an attitude to "make do." As a young woman, she left her island life to become a nun and follow a teaching career in schools run by her congregation throughout Newfoundland. Her views of early life and community seem somewhat coloured by her many years in a religious community. She saw a great deal of order in her early life, and a purpose for everything. This, more than anything else, has given her a strong sense of discipline in her feelings for commitment, community cooperation and order. Few negative aspects of early life are mentioned, although the hardships are made clear. There was always someone or something to meet every need. She saw a certain acceptance of illness, disease, and death as belonging to the natural order of life.

Her remarks provoke comment on some issues specific to health and illness. Infant mortality was high in rural Newfoundland during the early part of this century. Diphtheria took its toll and the narrator notes an interesting belief about germs remaining viable behind wall paper. Social isolation was a problem. Most outports had no road access to larger communities with doctors and cottage hospitals. Babies and children often had to be brought by open boat across considerable distances, taking hours by sea. An alternative was to wait for the coastal schooner, the principal means of travel, but it came only once or twice a month. One could also send for the district nurse; again, travel time was a factor.

We see, too, a sense of self-sufficiency in looking after their own regarding illness and death. This was extended, as well, to looking after their neighbours without having to be asked. In their small communities they responded to need wherever it existed. If this informant shows any regrets over her life, it is only for failure to question events and for being too accepting: "I didn't question my mother, my parents much. In those days we never did." That parents and others in authority were respected and their decisions rarely directly challenged were part of some people's self-discipline.

●

I was born on February 16, 1899, at Red Island, Placentia Bay. My father was born in that area, but my mother came from Bristol's Cove, a country place just outside Harbour Grace. I don't know when mother moved to Red Island, but she grew up at Harbour Grace. My mother went teaching in Red Island and met my father. He was her second husband. She had one child and my father was married and had three. They got together, married, and produced my family. They already had four before we came along. I'm the only one living now. Agnes was the oldest, she died when she was four of diphtheria that was raging in the area then. I can't remember her. I was next. I was the second. Then my brother Tom, and there were two babies in between, Theresa and Rita. They died at about eight months, and the last of the family was Rose. I remember going to the graveyard with these two babies, Rita and Theresa.

Never knew she had a heart condition

The last then was Rose. It's eleven years between myself and her. She was seventy-six when she died. She had a heart condition. Nobody knew she had it. She went through her childhood and her school life and her life in religion as a teacher. Never knew she had a heart condition. Her death came almost suddenly. Three weeks before her death she was able to drive to her nephew's funeral. Three weeks! It only happened in that length of time.

I didn't question my mother, my parents much

I don't know what Rita and Theresa died of. I didn't question my mother, my parents much. In those days we never did. All of us older people regret that we hadn't asked more questions. I really don't know what they died of. Another thing is, there was no doctor or nurse on the island. We looked after our own as far as the ordinary illnesses. But, of course, if anything like diphtheria—that was before my day—I presume there was a doctor over there to pronounce it diphtheria anyway.

I don't know how many families lived there then, but at one time there were about five hundred people, and it was thriving. I also remember some of the women on the island not belonging there, and I asked my mother, "How did these women come to be here?" They weren't born on the island. Like Mrs. Ryan was from Holyrood and Mrs. Barry was from Fermeuse. She said they came up here to work.

Merasheen Island was larger. But the harbour where the people lived was on the south of that island, not on the Red Island side either. We were on the east side. But if we went to Merasheen, you had to go right around and come over the harbour and it was very rough at times. I used to hear the fishermen say it was very rough going into Merasheen Harbour and I was seasick.

When we were children

When we were children, of course, we played all the children's games. Playing jacks, and, if you couldn't afford to buy marbles, we got them in the beach. You picked out the ones small enough, five I think. I wouldn't know how to play it now. Wintertime, outdoors, we did a lot of sliding, not much skating. There wasn't any near place to skate. There was a lot of hills on Red Island.

We had dancing and, Christmas time, mummering. I remember as a child dressing up. Myself and my brother, growing up, he would have my clothing on and I would have his. But only as a child. But I remember mummers coming in; they were dressed up and you were trying to guess who they were.

As children you had to take whatever was going. There was no such thing as saying, "I don't like this." Whatever was cooked you had to take it. That meant you got a balanced meal all the time. You had different vegetables, then you had peas and beans and lots of rabbits. That would be mostly in the winter.

There was real community spirit there

There was real community spirit there. And there was no such thing as going to a person's house and ringing the door bell. When you went to a person's house, you walked in. When I was entering the Convent, I didn't think anything of it at the time. I visited every house in the harbour to say goodbye to them. Usually I got some kind of a little gift, but I didn't really do it for that. One old lady, I can see her now. She always reminded me of Queen Victoria from her pictures. She was in her room all the time, but the family were very good to her. She gave me a silk handkerchief. That was special. She treasured it, I suppose.

Another thing I remember is how they helped each other. For instance, if a family was burnt out, a couple of the men took it on themselves to go all around the harbour for contributions for the family. I remember seeing the two men in my mind; they're both dead now.

The same way with people who were sick or dying, certain women in the place would go around. Espe-

cially if the person was dying, they go over for Mrs.
Dunphy or Mrs. Reddy or so on, and be there because
the priest wouldn't be there. You couldn't go across
Placentia Bay for the priest, for the person who was
dying. But he'd come on the missions, and visit these
sick people, and give the sacraments.

My niece told me when she was up visiting me the
other day; she had some friend in St. John's who was
telling her the same thing about growing up on Red
Island. She said, "It seems you had a very happy life
growing up there." She said, "I wouldn't trade it for
anything." She spent thirty-five years in Montreal,
and she's been all around the province. She's a telegram operator.

The fishery, that's all the industry there was

The fishery, that's all the industry there was—that's
why it was inhabited anyway. They say the good
fishing grounds were on the island. My father was
much older than my mother, so in my day when I was
growing up, my father was more of a supervisor. He
didn't go out to the fishing grounds or anything like
that. He was too old for that I would say, and he would
supervise the making of the fish. My brothers went
fishing; my mother's first child, and then there was
one boy in this middle family. They're both dead now.

In those days the fish wasn't sold fresh, it was always
made and dried and sold. Where it was sold in my
day, I can't remember. I know later on it was sold to a
firm in Harbour Buffett, where Wareham's had a big
fishery business. My father did that with the fish from
around the island, the harbour, from the smaller
boats. I can see him down on the wharf now, culling
the fish, grading it. There was about four grades.
Then some merchant would come and take it up,
perhaps to Harbour Buffett, down the bay from Red
Island. Although every spring my father used to come

down alone on business and dealt with Bowrings a lot for the equipment and that it wasn't a holiday.

But I forgot to say that he had two boats, not large boats, sailboats, of course, in those days. He must have had them before he married my mother because they are called after his first family. The *John Thomas*, that was the boy that died, he called the boat after him, and the *Annie*, who was his eldest daughter. Now I can't remember the *Annie* as far as going fishing. I remember the *John Thomas*, they'd go out to Cape St. Mary's, anyone that had a large boat.

It always strikes me. It'll tell you how childish I was, in the middle of the summer, the skipper and three or four men would be the crew. In the middle of the summer they arrived home, the boat had wrecked out around St. Bride's. When I think of it now, what a loss that was to my father and these men. I must have been young at the time; it didn't concern me much. It was only when I grew up, especially since I got older, to think they ran into some of the rough places coming from Cape St. Mary's. They had to come up the Cape Shore. I can see the men now, four men, in the middle of a nice summer day with no boat. Luckily they survived.

The other boat, the *Annie*, I don't remember her gone fishing. All I remember her, freighting, bringing freight from St. John's. I suppose they brought fish down, but I don't know. Now there's no one old enough for me to talk to about that. My two brothers are dead. The oldest one I have is a cousin; she's eighty-seven. She married in Fox Harbour but she might have known if she was over visiting.

Like the *Annie*, I can't remember that boat fishing. I remember the other one that was wrecked. Later on, Jim, my half brother, when he was old enough to man a boat, he took charge of the *Annie*. He had two men with him freighting down from Red Island to St. John's. They'd call in at other ports, especially in rough weather. The last time they were freighting they were in Fermeuse Harbour. I think it was October. They called it the October Gale; they call it hurricanes now. They were anchored in the harbour in Fermeuse and the storm was so terrible the anchor broke. They were carried right out to sea, and in those days, at that particular time a lot of them brought out on account of the storm. Their anchors weren't heavy enough to hold them there. People in Fermeuse couldn't do anything about it. They could see them being driven out, out on mid-Atlantic. My brother was held on to his rosary beads. On the deck they had the rosary; they were tumbling around. It was a sailboat, and he was washed overboard. Held on to his rosary. The other men, of course, being hardy fishermen, threw him a rope and got him.

The government had a cutter out to search for these boats that were driven out. But there was no sign of it. A big ship, a passenger ship as far as I understand, they hailed to them and got no response. That was always a little mark against that firm, whoever owned that big steamer. So later on they came across another one and they hailed to them. I can remember the name of her, the *Mandinock*, big passenger steamer going to England and answered their call. They said they couldn't change their course but could take them on board. My brother told us they didn't care where they were going as long as they were saved. But now what were they going to do with their own boat, so they had to set it on fire so it wouldn't be a menace to navigation. That was the *Annie*. They were on their way to England when the cutter caught up with them on this big steamer and they transferred them. They got home that way.

In the meantime, I was in school in Littledale and didn't know anything about it. Jim came to see me before he went home. He was about a month home when this little small package came to him. And it was his rosary beads that he left in the berth on the big steamer. Got it from the Captain. I was home at that time on my holidays. I can see the card of the Captain. He sent back the beads and his card. Of course, we say that it was Our Lady that protected him. God protected him through Our Lady's intercession. He was washed overboard and they pulled him in out in mid-Atlantic, only three of them. They weren't fishing; they were freighting between the bay and St. John's. We certainly had faith. In those days you'd be wondering what happened to these beads; they'd be a relic now in somebody's archives. Nobody ever thought of things like that then.

That'll tell you, a miracle through devotion to Our Lady. He still held on to his rosary beads; he must have put them in his pocket or something. He saved them. And he was saved through the intercession of Our Blessed Lady, certainly. Also it was God's will that he be saved. He's dead now, but he married, had a family. Some of the family are living now. You know Judge McCarthy? That was his son. My father was alive then. He died suddenly about two years after I entered the convent.

The family rosary was a regular thing

We had the rosary, the family rosary was a regular thing, and in school we had to learn our catechism. Question and answer, and you'd get a red star for all the questions you answered correctly.

Then, on Sundays, of course, being on an island, there was no priest there. In those days, if you didn't have a priest for Mass, but you had the rosary in the church. The men from the community, I can see Mr. Garrett Ryan now with his whisker going up Sunday mornings. Now, instead of Mass, Mr. Ryan would come over for the rosary.

You would no more miss that rosary than you would miss Mass on Sundays. All those who could go were there, everyone in the place. I don't remember anyone staying away unless it was too far away. There was some coves on the island where some people lived apart from the harbor too. There were families living down there and they'd have to walk. It was a nice distance.

With religion, of course, your mother looked after your prayers, taught you your prayers. As soon as I was able to read I remember my mother putting a prayer book into my hands and telling me what prayers to say. Whether you'd call it prayers or not. Then I became fond of praying. I remember some of the long prayers that I used to say, but I don't know now because we have the Office, the liturgy of the Office.

I liked to pray. That might be contributory to my vocation, I suppose, to be fond of prayer. But I got that from my parents really. You had a long stretch of grace before and after meals. You wouldn't dare do without that.

I did have diphtheria when I was about twelve

I'm healthy. I was healthy all my life. One time, I was sitting next to a neighbour on Red Island and I was saying how healthy I was. She said, "Sure, your mother was healthy." I don't remember my mother being sick except when the babies were coming along. She had chest trouble all right. Otherwise, she was never in bed, to my knowledge, of any sickness except when the children were born.

I did have diphtheria when I was about twelve. My oldest sister had it years and years before that. I was in Placentia with my half-sister who was married in there. Nobody knows where I got it. Nobody in Placentia had it. There was an old house being torn down. In those days all the papering, sometimes they wouldn't take the paper off. They'd paper on top of what was there before, and there'd be layers of it. I went past that house every day to go to the post office, used to go to the post office every day. Some thought perhaps some germs came from that. This is what people were thinking, as far as I remember now. In those days you made your paste and used that to put on the paper. You didn't buy glue and it wasn't on the paper. I can see my mother with the pail of paste now.

Probably my system was run down

That time in my life too, I suppose, developing adolescence, probably my system was run down. I wasn't bad with it either. I had a couple days of a cold before the doctor decided it was diphtheria. I had a sore throat; I couldn't swallow. He came over and gave me the antitoxin. That's what they called it in those days. Put a needle in my back. I suppose it was an antibiotic; something they had for it, for diphtheria in those days. But I wasn't bad with it at all.

There was a family spirit there. One elderly lady, Gran Reddy, we used to call her. Anyone got cut or anything else of that sort, the child would be brought over to Gran Reddy's. What she had in her, I don't know, but she'd look after it. Stopping blood or something, she used to do. I don't know what she did but you called her the "doctor of the island." It wasn't by charm she did it. There was no religious connection to what she did. No, there was none of that. The Catholic faith was too strong for that. And, in mind, she was kind of a leader too in the community. She looked after everyone's interests.

The Lord provides

The Lord provides in cases like that. You have no doctor, yet look at the very few babies that died. You had the midwife there, an elderly lady. You believed in her. She knew what to do. Where she learned it, we don't know.

Wherever there are children there are going to be accidents. Children were always running around, falling into the water. There was no such thing as First Aid. Fish them out of the water and get them going again. If they had cuts, especially larger cuts, bleeding that they couldn't control, you tend to it. I remember children being down around the wharf where the men were cutting fish. They'd have special knives, and sometimes these children, mischievous, would be around and fall on a knife or something and perhaps get cut by somebody's knife. It happened, they'd wrap the child up and bring her up to Mrs. Reddy. Now, I don't remember her medicines or what she'd do with it, but I know she was very interested in every family.

Then the economy, if people economized, I think there's a lot of waste now. I remember my brother, children in the outports getting the bread and molasses. You'd be out playing and come in and your mother would give you a slice of homemade bread and molasses. That was a part of our good health. Some would ask for bread and butter and molasses, but my mother said "no," we couldn't have butter and molasses. It would be a waste, you see. You had to economize. The same with clothing; you patched your clothing and you did all your sewing. There was no such thing as buying something from a factory, I suppose, until the catalogue came along.

You had faith in your doctor then

You have access to a doctor now. There's nobody living there now anyways but the people that go over there fishing. They live in Placentia or somewhere else. It's a different world altogether as far as the outports, different times, different age. You have more access to doctors and nurses and hospitals now. Then, with the roads, everywhere you go now there's a paved road.

I suppose you had faith in your doctor then, and as far as I'm concerned you have faith in the doctor now. In those days especially, the doctor was somebody who could do something for you. In my family, anyway, they had faith in the doctor. You only had the General Practitioner. If you went to him he couldn't give you much, only general medication. Perhaps some of the older people would sense that and not think they were getting the best. As far as he was concerned, it was the best he could do. The mind has a lot to do with the body. They used to say that in the San, years ago. "Be cheerful; it helps." Whatever your attitude is your spirit is; it helps your bodily health too.

Mr. Abe Davis, b. 1913, Conception Bay

Our second narrative is from a man born into a large family on the northern shore of the Avalon Peninsula, at Seal Cove, Conception Bay. There were four boys and four girls. Typical of the north shore, they were of the Anglican faith. His recollections convey a strong sense of a life constrained by work and limited material resources.

The early years of his working life were spent as a labourer, finding a job wherever one was available. Generally, this meant leaving home to find work elsewhere. His first job was as a farm helper on Bell Island. Later on, he was a tractor-trailer driver for a few years, before establishing himself as a shopkeeper. This provided a reasonably comfortable living for himself and his first and second wives. He lost his first in childbirth.

This narrative describes little of the bright side of life often met in accounts from those raised on the Southern Shore. Nevertheless, family life seemed cohesive and ordered, and not without entertainment. Forced into work at age fifteen, his happy memories were often overshadowed by the harsh realities of living in rural Newfoundland. Neither man nor God brought much relief to him and his family during the Depression, "on the dole was six cents a day, and nothing, only black flour."

Nutrition, or rather malnutrition, stands out in his comments relating to health. One sister, he believes, died of malnutrition. The informant believes the same might have happened to him had not the English minister interfered while visiting his house and insisted on better care for the boy. Nourished by a glass of milk with a beaten egg in it each day, he recovered. The comment that the diagnosis of "lumbago" was an euphemism for malnutrition raises interesting questions about the stigma attached to poverty. As in our first narrative infant mortality is again an issue.

●

I was born here in Seal Cove. There was eight of us altogether, four brothers and four sisters. It was rough. You never had half enough to eat. What you did have to eat was probably—lots of time it was dry bread, tea with no sugar in it, like that. Yes, molasses in your tea, molasses on your bread. No kind of fruit unless an apple from an old apple tree that fell, yes, old crab apple. You'd get an apple probably, Christmas, that was all and a few common candy. That was all you'd get. A scattered one in our family got a mouth organ in their stocking, or some other little toy. The bigger the family you had the harder it was, less to eat, that kind of stuff.

I remember when I was growing up on the dole was six cents a day and nothing, only black flour. You had to blow out the lamp in the night; you couldn't keep it burning. Only a bit of wood in the stove, no kind of insulation in the houses or no kind of heat at all. And by nine o'clock the fire was gone out and the lamp was gone out. You had about fifteen rocks on the stove to take to bed. You'd be afire then with rocks and bricks and that kind of stuff. When it got cold you'd strike your toe off it. It would fall on the floor then, out of the bed.

You never had no place to go in growing up, or nothing like that, just walking around the road or in the woods. Yes, or in the garden setting vegetables, stuff like that, all summer long. You'd get out fishing with your father. We used to use the spot across the river. Some fellow would get playing the mouth organ. You had to be home in the bed nine o'clock; there was no electricity then only lamps. They couldn't afford to keep the light going in the lamp any longer than nine o'clock. Mostly had the violin and the accordion; that's all that was around here then. There'd always be one or two people there to play the accordion or the violin.

You couldn't buy nothing then

My father was never sick in his life. He was eighty-six when he died. He fished for awhile, then he worked in North Sydney for awhile in the coal mines. And he worked on Bell Island in the iron ore mines. I'd be doing all the work in the woods and doing the gardens, growing vegetables, stuff like that. Everyone, I think, everyone had their own garden, small garden on the back of their house, enough to grow enough for the winter.

Most everybody used to have probably a horse and a cow. Some would probably have two or three sheep, more or less to get the wool for knitting. Knit mitts you see, mitts and socks for the winter. Yes, they grew their own hay to feed the cattle. You couldn't buy nothing then. You could buy it but people didn't have the money.

I went to work at fifteen years old on a farm over on Bell Island. Five years on the farm, I was twenty then. I worked before doing little odd jobs, on the highroads; get a month in the summer; or get a month on the railroad. Mr. Murphy I worked for. He had fourteen cows and a couple of horses, one to deliver the milk and one to work on the ground. I used to do all that work myself. Get up four-thirty in the morning and start milking the cows. And then I'd bring in the full bucket of milk into the house, and Mrs. Murphy used to bottle it then. She didn't scald it,

right from the cow to the customer. She used to bottle
it up in regular quart bottles with the seal and all on
it. Yes, I used to bring it in and she would bottle it up,
and that's all there was to it. She'd pasteurize some
just to get the cream off it.

When they were small, I remember rocking my
brothers and sisters in the cradle. Mother would say,
"Sit on the cradle and rock this one to sleep." Perhaps
she'd make a tit to put in his mouth. Tie a bit of fine
cloth with a bit of bread in it and tie a string around it
and shove it in the molasses. Put that in his mouth and
that would keep him quiet while I rocked him to
sleep. Once in a while he'd haul it out and throw it on
the floor. I'd pick it up and stick it back in his mouth
again. That didn't make him sick. I've often shook
them off and put it back in his mouth; that didn't
make him sick. The doctor would put you in hospital
if you told him that.

Oh, yes, the flies used to pitch on him and I've
often brushed them off. No such thing then as string
wire for flies. If there was a fly at all, he was in the
house. No screen doors or windows then. Yes, while
she'd be washing or baking—you had to bake every
bit of bread in the oven—she'd also look after the
small ones. Oh, yes, and in the gardens, sometimes
milk the cow, bring the milk in and scald it.

She used to make the salve...and put it on the cut

One of the children cut his hand with a knife or
something. My grandmother sent me in the woods
with a cup, to a var tree with a big bladder on it. I squat
the turpentine out of it in a can and bring it out. She
used to make salve out of that and put it on the cut.

I think there were a couple of brothers or sisters
died before I was born. I know they had me give up
one time to die. The English minister every now and
then would visit the congregation, probably once a
month. I remember I was only in the house with the

kitchen light on and I couldn't get up out of it. And when he came in the house he said, "Liz (my mother's name), what's wrong with the boy?" She said, "I don't know, he's sick like that a week or longer." He come over and started feeling my ribs and he said, "That boy is sick." He said, "He got lumbago, have you got any milk?" We never had no milk at that time. He said, "Give him a glass of milk a day and put a beat up egg into it." And in one week I was just as well as I is today. That's what he called it. I heard him tell my mother that I wouldn't have lived much longer if they didn't do that. I must have been six or seven years old then.

That's what they called it, lumbago

That's what they called it, lumbago. Just starving, hungry, no nourishment at all. I remember when he was going out through the door, he said to my mother, "I'm coming back in two days time and he better be feeling better." So he did, come back two days after and checked on me. One sister died, I think that's what happened to her. She was six or eight years old, that's what I'd say she died from. That's right. That's what she died of, she was acting the very same way too. Just weak, that's all, I couldn't even get up.

I heard the minister tell as he went to the porch: "Good thing I came along or he'd a been dead in another couple of days time," he said. Yes, a lot of people died. You couldn't see a doctor.

It's just whatever your luck was

Two of my sisters went in service. Two died when they were eight, ten years old. Two lived and they are still living yet. One is eighty-three and the other is seventy-one. They mostly worked out around on the farms on Topsail Road. Cowans had a farm, and there was Jack on the Mount Pearl side. There was a lot of farms out there then. Girls that went into service worked mostly on farms, yes. It's just whatever your luck was. You had no experience then for nothing. Everyone was alike, you didn't have to be particular then. They start probably twelve, fourteen years old, around there and worked until they got married. Yes, knew all about housework, do stuff, sewing, that's all. Take in a lot of sewing. Making coats, overalls, caps and everything.

Housework, get anywhere from three to four dollars a month doing housework. Minnie can tell you. She went to work for four dollars a month. Just ordinary housework they had to do. The same on the farm, just farm work. No machinery then, not like you got today, just a horse and plough. Do nothing, only in the house, that's all. Pretty good, some places had washers, the regular old fashioned washer. They use to like it; it was interesting. There was lots of everything and good food when you were there. That's right. Even if it was only four dollars or five dollars, there was nowhere to spend it. You couldn't spend it hardly.

The earlier days was better

The earlier days was better than they ended off in the '20s. It was better in 1930 than it was in the '20s. Oh, yes, cutting wood all day long, rails for your fence. Oh, yes, everybody had to cut their own.

Now you always got a dollar in your pocket. I remember my grandmother, she used to get five dollars every three months from the government. She had to be seventy-five years old to get that. She used to give us all a nickel every three months. We'd go up to the store and get it changed in coppers. Then you'd go buy some common candy out of it. She'd give you a handful. She'd say give me your pocket, and take a handful and drop it in your pocket. For one cent, you'd have enough for all day.

You had to go to church, that was it. Sunday school in the evening, used to have Sunday school every single evening, and go to church after supper. Most everyone, you had to walk about three miles to go church. Oh, yes, you had to go. You couldn't get away from it. You might get a stick when you come home if you missed it. Mother used to go. My father, he didn't go very much. On Sundays, all you were allowed to do was probably take the horse up to the river to water him. Each Sunday, you had to clean on Saturday, get a shave and a wash and peel all your potatoes and turnip and cabbage. All that had to be done on Saturday. Sunday morning you had a change of clothes, change our underwear, that'd be the first thing.

We'd do some visiting like that. Just walk around the road, meet some of your friends. We couldn't do anything on Sunday, no way. That was strictly out, no kind of games on Sunday. We used to play jacks, with marbles, and see how many jacks you could catch on the back of your hand. You could do that on Sunday evening, sit out by the door on the grass and do that. We kept our good clothes on all day. Like if you had to do anything like feed the cattle or water the cattle, you'd take your good clothes off then. Wouldn't even shave, would shave Saturday night. Cook dinner, that's all she'd do.

If you wanted anything, just sing out

If you wanted anything, just sing out. If you wanted to shift a shed, just sing out. Maybe four or five men would come and help you do it. No one could pay anything. So I would go to you and you would come to us. Yes, they'd be all coming to visit you and bring you something.

The work is different altogether now, they got everything to do it with. Then it had to be done with a pick and shovel or wheelbarrow or take it on your back and lug it. Everything in the house now is push button. And your cars and the trucks got everything to do your work with. You had nothing then but a horse and cart. I used to leave two o'clock in the morning. I take two and three barrels of carrot and potatoes on a horse and car, and walk to St. John's and sell them, all in the one day. Yes, it would take about five hours to walk out there with a horse and cart. It was all gravel roads then, not like now with pavement. Every hill was twice as steep as what it is now. They got them cut down now. We go around to people's houses selling vegetables. Somebody would go to the stores, sell them by the half gallon and the gallon. You'd have probably about ten dollars. No, you'd have five dollars for two barrels of potatoes. Some would sell splits, some selling fish, more selling potatoes, more selling turnip, everything, selling blueberries.

Go out with a load of splits, most everybody burned coal then. Even in St. John's, it was all coal then. Everybody lighting the fire every day, so sell a bag of splits in this house and another bag of splits in that house, like that. Sometimes you'd stay handy and people would come and buy it off you. The quickest way was to go door to door.

I don't think it's as good today. I wouldn't say. Children today, you got some bad ones but then it would be all, "Yes sir," "No sir." No, children was afraid then. Afraid of getting a beating or something. I used to be a big young fellow, get beat but there's no need of it. With a stick or something, the size of a picket three or four feet long probably across your back or legs. Oh, yes, brutal as far as I'm concerned. Some parents were really brutal. If it was today, they'd be all in the clink somewhere. No need of a lot of it. No, there was no law then at all. No, wouldn't interfere at all. It was no good to, no laws for that kind of stuff, not like today.

For keeping them clean and that kind of thing, they were good like that. But when they said, "Don't you go, you're not going." You didn't and you didn't talk back either. If you did, you'd know what you were going to get when you came back in the house. Some mothers was good and more fathers was good. Not very often you'd get the two of them bad. Some, probably the mother had no patience and in the other house probably the man didn't have no patience. You was drove to bed probably for the rest of the day and kept there for all day and all night.

She had eight children

My first wife, she died at thirty-six years old. She had eight children. There was one born; she borned him. Three years after I met the other woman. She was lucky because I was working the same time too. They always tried to put me on a night shift so I could be home by day to look after them. She reared them. She died when she was only fifty-eight.

Pregnancy wasn't talked about. Funny about that, isn't it? You weren't allowed to say nothing like that anyway. Oh! We came up from under a rock or the stork brought us. Brought by the stork or someone got he out under a rock. We used to do a lot of matting then, I remember this woman, I used to hear my mother talking about her, her stomach would swell up from matting, up against the mat frame. Some married because of pregnancy. Abortion, no, nothing like that unless it was a miscarriage or something like that. It never happened; it was never talked about anyway.

I don't do too much driving around town

I'm 79 years old see and I don't do too much driving around town, only around Topsail Road. The other day, I had to turn left to go to Topsail Road. As I turned to go down, I had to get over on the left with the arrow. I was on the arrow and there was two cars

ahead of me and they started to go. The first one went
on and this other one, he got halfways across and he
stopped. He started to come back. I didn't know what
to do and I cut around him and went on. That's all I
thought about it.

When I got almost down to Powers Court I happened to look in the glass and I see a light flashing. I
said, "That's a police car coming down there." I
pulled in because I thought he wanted to go on and
they stopped behind me. I said, "What have I done
now, I wonder." He pulled in behind me and he got
out and come up to me. Kind of a half smile on his
face, he said, "What did you do up there?" I said,
"What do you think I done?" "I don't know, I can't
figure out what you done," he said. I told him, "I
passed on the arrow. The car ahead of me stopped
and I hauled out around him." He said, "It looked
something like that, but I wasn't sure."

He asked me for my license and said, "How long
have you had a license?" I said "I had my first license
in 1933." He looked at them and smiled and I said,
"Do you know what, I never had a ticket of no kind in
my life yet." No, and he said "You're not going to get
one now." When he left he wished me goodbye, but he
said, "I don't know what you did it for, but don't do it
anymore." He laughed as he was going.

Mrs. Roberta Haynes, b. 1921, Labrador

The third narrative is from a woman raised in southern
Labrador. Her recollections of her early life are generally
very positive and reflect an even more self-sufficient lifestyle
than the previous two. One of eight children, she grew up in
St. Michael's Bay where she eventually married. She remained in the same community most of her life and raised
three children of her own. Only in her retirement years did
she come down to the northern peninsula of Newfoundland
to live.

The sense of family unity and identity revealed in the narrative was an essential part of the way of the life she describes. Life in southern Labrador was good; plentiful fish, game, and other food contributed to self-sufficiency. It seemed better than that on the southern shore with its closer access to the fishing grounds. Our informant is proud of her personal accomplishments as a woman. She fished, hunted and trapped for food and skins to turn into clothing. Reaping nature was just as much a way of life for her as it was for her brothers. What else could a young woman do in a family of six girls and one boy?

Self-sufficiency is a strong theme throughout this narrative. Father was frequently at the traps; wood had to be cut and hauled. Yet, evening brought quieter moments for crochet, games and school work. Illnesses and pregnancies were all part of life; accidents were dealt with as a matter of course. Tonics and medicines were as often homemade as bought. Old people and midwives were the common health care experts. We see, too, a sense of deep spirituality. Despite infrequent visits from a clergyman, they prayed as a family and sought support and encouragement from within. They were strongly self-sufficient, and thankful for what they got from nature.

●

I was born in St. Michael's Bay, Labrador, and I grew up there. Mother was born and grew up in George's Cove, Labrador, and dad down at North West River, down by Goose Bay. He grew up there until he was a young man. And then they went to Port Blandford and lived for five or six years. His Dad didn't want to go back trapping on the Labrador, so he and his brother went back trapping. And after they was back for a few years, his father and mother decided, if their two sons were going to stay on the Labrador and trap, catch fur, they'd go back to Labrador to live. So they all went back and built a house in the head of St.

Michael's Bay, which Dad lived there 50 years in the
one settlement.

When I was growing up I had six sisters and one
brother. He was the baby. In St. Michael's Bay there
was lots of fur and rabbits and partridges to catch. I
used to have traps out myself, me and my sister. I've
caught a fox and I caught a mink and I caught a lot of
muskrats and squirrels and weasels and that kind of
thing. Yes, I used to like that. Hunting and fishing was
the way you'd make your money. There wasn't any
other way to make money, only go fishing or catching
fur, when I was young.

Even Mom would get out and help dry the fish on the flake

We used to play football, what we called it. We used to
snowshoe race and run and have rabbit snares out.
Sometimes we'd take a lantern by night to go and look
at our snares and get a rabbit would be right exciting.
In the summertime we'd pick berries. We'd go and
haul herring nets and get herring and clean them,
and go and jig fish and clean that and salt it and dry
it. Then we'd sell it to make a little bit of money for
ourselves. But you'd only get $2.50 a quintal then and
there's a lot of fish in a quintal. We were all involved
as a family, whatever one done. Even Mom would get
out and help dry the fish on the flake. She didn't go
out in the boat like we used to.

When we were out working, Mom would be cooking and have a good meal cooked for when we came
home, when we were out in the boat. And in the
winter we'd be going in the woods. Daddy used to go
away and be gone perhaps a week or two weeks or
longer on the trap line, to his traps. We had to get all
the wood. Go in the woods and cut it and haul it home,
and then saw it up to the door. I loved outdoor work
when I was young.

We were a close family, always happy. Days when it
was too stormy in the wintertime to get out to do this

kind of work, we'd be doing fine work, doing pillow-cases and lunch cloths and things like that. Some-times we'd be able to sell 'em and make a little money that way. We would sell them to people over in Port Hope Simpson, when we'd go over there. Some peo-ple liked to buy things like that, pillowcases, crochet. To go there by dog team, like we used to go when I was home, was 40 miles. In the wintertime, when we couldn't get out quite as much, we'd make skin boots, and in the night we'd play games. We'd play checkers, and hide-and-go-seek, and dominoes, and all those kinds of games. The nights would go quick, because there wasn't very many families when I was growing up, only four in the head of St. Michael's Bay.

I only had part of two years going to school. But I could read and write. I went in grade two when I went to school because Mom and Dad made us write, do our letters and read, taught us to read and write. They got us to copy letters, and letters to write off, things so that they wanted us to know how to read and write. You'd have to go away to Grenfell school in Cart-wright if you wanted to get schooling. Mom always said if we went away from home she wanted us to be able to write, to write letters home and be able to read letters if she wrote to us.

Mom was a good help for Daddy getting the logs

Mother, she worked as a servant, a maid, for a short while before she was married. Probably the woman was expecting and had a small baby and needed someone for a while to come in and do some work. Mom was a good help for Daddy getting the logs. I can remember when I was a child growing up, Mom would be down at the stage when they'd get a lot of fish and probably wouldn't get it put away, the fish done, until one o'clock in the night. And I'd be up home rocking the cradle. Mom told me she often came in and seen me sound asleep on the floor and

my hand still on the cradle when I'd be rocking the
baby. I'd sooner be out of doors trying to make money
that way, working. I went probably for two or three
days and work like that. But I'd sooner be jigging the
fish and catching the fish and drying it and get stuff
for myself.

My mother, she was a midwife

If anyone got sick, you'd go and do what you could.
Go and help out, help one another and do the best
they could. My mother, she was a midwife. She borned Ivy, my oldest daughter. Yes, she was a midwife
for years, after she got her own family just about
grown up.

And her mother was a midwife for years before her.
She borned an awful lot of babies, Grandmother
Penney. Mom's father was from Newfoundland. She
was born down in Labrador, because he married a girl
from Labrador and lived down there. Mother became
a midwife after her own family was born. The doctors
and nurses wasn't there, so midwives had to do the
work. And they used to have to go around. If those
small communities didn't have a midwife, in the fall
before the Bay would freeze up and afraid it wouldn't
be froze up enough to get a midwife, then they'd take
the midwife. Perhaps she'd have to stay a couple of
months, waiting, if there was no midwife in the settlement.

I can remember when my cousin chopped one finger off

Now, if we get sick, we'll go to a doctor right away. But
then, when we were home, we'd just depend on the
old midwives and the older people for their cures. I
can remember when my cousin, she was the same age
as I, chopped one finger off and the other almost off.
There was no one there to do anything in the head of
the Bay in the fall. Mom and Grandmother done that.
They took the finger, it was hanging off, just a little bit

of skin, and they put it on and done it up, and fixed the other one. But her brother bumped it, and made it a little bit crooked after they had it done up. But after, when the doctor came and seen it, they said that Mom and Grandmother did a really good job. You wouldn't think about touching that today, would you? You'd have to go to a hospital with anyone with a finger chopped off and the other one half chopped off. One was chopped right off. Just hanging with a bit of skin, but it was straight when they put it on. They put it on and it grew on, never turned to blood poison or anything. They saved her two fingers, but it couldn't buckle.

They used that stuff off the trees, called turpentine. And they used to put that on those cuts and that was really good for healing. You'd disinfect the bandage, burn it, brown it. You'd put it on the stove, put something clean down, or even go to work brown flour on a clean piece of rag and that was right good. The same as they had like iodine and Friars Balsam, and they used that kind of stuff too. They had their own medicine, but a lot of it they got from going and get this turpentine and save it up in bottles, and all their own medicine. They said cod oil was good too.

Mom used to render out cod livers

In the summer Mom used to render out cod livers and wash and clean and then bottle it up. In the winter we used to have to drink cod oil and put it on our chest with a little bit of Minard's Liniment into it. When we'd get a cold a piece of flannelette was put on your chest and on your back and it seemed like it really done good. And when you'd get a sore throat, you'd take the stocking off your left foot and put it around your neck. I've done that a good many times, because they used to say it was a cure in the stocking of your left foot and it seemed like it done the job.

Spruce boughs . . . it would give you a good appetite

They used to go to work and steep out spruce boughs. Get spruce boughs, clean boughs, and wash them and steep them out and then drain off the water. The liquor was put in bottles. Take a drink, it would give you a good appetite. The dogwood rind would clean your blood, and things like this we would do. In the morning you were supposed to take the dogwood. The same way you were supposed to take a spoonful of cod liver oil in the morning, to keep your lungs healthy. They used to tell us that. We'd take it every day, mostly in the springtime. That's when Dad and Mom believed you could get run down and get sick. You wouldn't get sick so quick, they believed. And you were not supposed to eat a lot of greasy foods. And do walking. Most everyone did walking, but they said that was healthy. Because, if you didn't walk very much, and when you started to walk, your breath would be shorter.

Keep them dressed warm, good warm clothing. We had to listen good. We had to listen when we were told not to do anything, to endanger our life or anything. And we all had the rule put out for safe survival. To light a fire if we got astray, to not wander around through the woods. Light a fire and wait until some-one came. When we had our gun, fire three shots in the air in a row, then stop a while and fire three more. If people heard that they'd know you were in trouble.

About ten I started using a gun. I still got my own gun I used. Daddy had a new gun come from St. John's when I was a girl. We were all firing with it, but he said I could make the best shots. Somehow I had a knack for it I suppose. I was killing things better than my sisters. So the gun was given to me. And I got the gun to this day. When I went home one year, after Daddy was dead and Mom was still alive, she said, "Take your gun, your father give it to you, and take it

to Daniel's Harbour with you." So that's what I did
and I still got my gun today.

They never told us where babies came from. Those
things was all hid from us at those times. We figured
they come out of an old stump, an old rotten stump
they used to tell us when we were children growing
up. Not like today, they're not very old when they
know all those things. Oh, there's a lot of difference
now than it was then in my day. It don't seem to me
like it's happier, because we were happy then and that
was it. It seems like people are not so friendly, like
visiting, as they used to be in those days. But I suppose
it changed in a lot of ways because I drive a car now.

In our day you couldn't go to a doctor when you got
anything wrong with you. When I was a child growing
up with Mom and them, you had to go and get this
stuff that they were always told and what was used
from one generation to another. Well, now if we get
sick we'll go to a doctor right away. But then, when we
were home, we'd just depend on like the old midwives
and the older people for their cures. And there were
no planes flying then like it is today. In those outports
today, they'll take a patient and fly him to the hospital
or a doctor come in. But there was none of that. It was
rather go from where we lived to Cartwright. There
was a hospital there, and Mary's Harbour, there was a
hospital.

Mr. Albert Boland, b. 1921, Southern Shore

This last introductory narrative is from a man of very strong
character who bore his successes and failures with considerable determination. Important for him was a good relationship with his family, especially with those with whom he was
in business. He comes from a large family of Irish Catholic
descent from the southern shore of the Avalon Peninsula. As
was typical of older children in large families, he was denied
what he wanted most—an education. He accepted this as part
of his time and place, but he never forgot the dream which he

eventually realized. The desire was so strong that when he was sixty years old he returned to school to complete his high school diploma.

Like our informant from Labrador, this man reflects a firm sense of independence and self-sufficiency. He had to make do with the resources around him. He had to make opportunities and seize luck quickly if it came his way. He also had to know when to quit, when to move on, and when to start over again. The money to be made was in exporting fish all over the world, especially to Japan in recent years.

By all appearances a successful man from humble beginnings, he expresses no bitterness. Those were the times and that was the life. He accepted the things he could not change, and made a 'damned fine' attempt to change what he could. He made many changes in his lifetime, living a varied and full life.

Apart from his open acceptance of life as it was in his time, his family and himself, he placed particular emphasis on family. He tried hard to assuage and avert grievances within the family when divisions threatened. "Above anything else, I"ll never fall out with you and not talk to one another." Life was like that, you could not succeed in business if you were at odds with your partners. His comments enlarge our view of family struggles against difficult conditions. We learn how some families starved, and how some took tuberculosis to be the result.

●

Born in Bay Bulls May 1921, I was the first child borned by Dr. Whelan when he arrived here. I was the fourth child of nine: six brothers and three sisters. Mother and father were born in Bay Bulls. They both grew up in Bay Bulls. My mother went to school in St. Mary's, Halifax, for a while; and my father went to school in Bay Bulls. My mother was a housewife, before that I have no idea what she did.

I had to leave school . . . in order to survive

She went to St. Mary's College in Halifax. My father had different jobs in Depression days. He was a mail courier, and he had a contract from St. John's to Tors Cove and delivered the mail twice a week to the post offices along the way, winter and summer. He had a contract for a year, sometimes two years, he had to have a truck and a horse and different kinds of carts and sleds to qualify for the contract. His wages were $70 a month and it was very, very hard to support a family of nine children. It was a starvation wage; there was no doubt about it. So as we grew up, we had a local merchant in Bay Bulls, a fish merchant who employed a lot of young people and as young fellows we went to work very young. I went to work when I was thirteen years old.

I quit school because I had to go to work. I had to leave school at about grade three or four, I'm not sure, in order to survive. Because before that, before we worked, we had to live on a very, very tight budget and when it come to clothes, the boys didn't have anything to wear on their feet in the summertime, especially in my age, we went barefoot for June and July and August. We only had what we called sneakers to go to church with and we had to get a year out of those. And each winter we would get a pair of knee rubbers or hip rubbers and that was all very tight budget stuff.

We were only allowed to use a half a pound of sugar a day, a quarter pound of tea a day, one pound of butter a day. My mother would decide on that. If we used it all up in the morning there was no more sugar next morning, that was the way we had to live, we didn't want to go on relief or dole or whatever they called it, we stayed away from that.

Food got to come from somewhere

The other brothers came out a little bit better than
that because times were a little better; there wasn't as
many in the family, so as the family grew, the ex-
penses grew, if you follow me on that. We had to, we
also grew a lot of vegetables and cleared a lot of land,
and we had to have cows and horses and pigs and
sheep for our meat. That was all subsidizing his salary,
because when you get nine big, hardy eaters at a table,
the food got to come from somewhere, so we used a
lot of potatoes as food, a lot of cabbage as food, a lot
of turnip as food. Every year we would keep one pig
and we slaughter that sometime around Christmas,
and my father would salt some because there was no
refrigeration.

If it was an early winter he had a sled of his own
where he would put a beef barrel, a puncheon they
called it, molasses puncheon. Put ice in between and
it would keep the stuff frozen.

And mother, all night long, she knit socks and
gloves because that was a big demand, and she card
and spun her own wool.

There was no mercy in them.

Now we had a school system which I was very upset
over all my lifetime. Before I came along, we had male
teachers teaching the boys, and we had a priest that
came in and brought in a convent in here, brought in
the nuns, and there was no mercy in them. No, they
were selfish individuals. Whatever the priest wanted,
he got. I am saying the truth. They did nothing for the
boys. They went to bed at nine o'clock and they got up
at seven o'clock and started praying for something.
Instead of having us boys who worked ten hours a day,
at least go to school six hours a week in the night time;
they were only interested in the girls. If they were
considerate and thinking about what they were doing, they were only interested in the girls because the

girls couldn't work at the fish plant at those times. So they had nothing else to do, only help their mothers and go to school. The boys had to go to work and they couldn't go to school in the daytime. They made no provisions for us in the nighttime. The old priest was just as bad as they were.

The girls had much more of an opportunity to get through school. They went out in service somewhere in St. John's, or they went to the United States somewhere, or they went to school. There was nowhere else for them to go. We had to go do manual work, as hard as we could. And we were lucky to get jobs. People who were weaker than I was couldn't get a job. They looked at you, a scrawny young fellow. If you got the job, the other little runt, he didn't get it because he couldn't do the work.

I would have preferred to have had more of an opportunity in finishing school. As a matter of fact, I did that. I went to Mobile High School and got my grade eleven in the night. I was sixty years old.

A twenty million dollar volume

I was very successful. I worked hard all my life. I got managing a big business; I managed to turn a twenty million dollar volume. I built up nine fish plants. I was out at things all the time; I got my education. I got a system, my ego.

My older brother worked with my father at the mail and then got into freight service for the little stores. They would go to St. John's on a shopping spree and go back with ten bags of flour, five bags of sugar, and you'd get ten cents a bag or something. From then on, my father lost. He had a contract during the last election, 1930 or '31. Responsible Government we called it. He apparently talked too much about the candidates and the one he was supporting, the one he supported lost the election to the other guys. Away his job went. He was one and a half to two years without a contract, without a job. So then he had to go start a restaurant on Water Street, serving meals. My next brother went and worked with him.

It was just some kind of eleven, ten cents for a bowl of soup or whatever it was. We come back on Commission Government and he got his mail contract back. We held it after he died in 1943 or '44. We took it right on in big fashion from St. John's to Trepassey and we got extra trucks. We all worked as a family, not as a company but as a family. We all had trucks. I was seventeen when I got driving my own truck, my family truck. So then the Second World War came along and from there I never looked back.

I'd be wondering what was going on

But as far as health was concerned, we had only a midwife after the doctor went out of Bay Bulls. We had a midwife that borned all the babies. The doctor was here 'til he died, eight or ten years, or maybe twelve or fifteen years. I've forgotten myself. I was the first baby he borned. I remember a lot of my sisters and brothers being born by the midwife home in mother's bedroom. I'd be wondering what was going on. My mother would be fat and then she'd get thin again. They'd show you the new baby after a day or so. She'd stay in bed for nine days before she came downstairs.

The midwife would come in a kind of silent way. How is your mother? And she'd have a little suitcase like you got there and mother would be in bed. There'd be pans of water going upstairs and towels going upstairs and my father would be anxious. It would be all over my head. I don't remember anything.

The midwife would help around the house. There would be a kind of a little supper and she'd probably bring something nice with her. We'd have a can of bully beef or probably mustard pickles, a treat, and probably a tablecloth, a kind of celebration. She'd walk back to her home, which was nine miles. She'd be back every day until mother got well again. The midwife was paid. I would say, yes. It would be all according to the circumstances. If you couldn't afford it, she didn't charge. I'm sure that was the kind of a person she was. We went from that then to a visiting doctor. We had an old fellow by the name of Dr. Martin Cashin, come once a week for a little while. Then we were without doctors altogether for the longest while.

We grew up fast

My brothers and sisters were all born healthy I suppose. So there was no such thing as getting a doctor, not to my knowledge. They were all born healthy, thank God. We grew up fast. There is the whole family there behind you under the clock. That was taken two years ago, July. Since then, there's three of them died. I just got them together for that, really. I certainly did; I had a job. That's something that's hard to get together because of "I can't come today, but I can come tomorrow." I had a party at my summer place and I headed on out and had plenty of booze and food.

Let's finish off my brothers. Then the younger brother got his grade eleven because we were all earning money then. So he didn't have to work like I had to work. In the middle, I was. So he did very well and he finished his grade eleven in Bay Bulls. All the girls finished their grade eleven. They married, two married servicemen out here in Mount Pearl.

Those years were good years

We all worked together. Those years were good years. We knew what the Depression was all about and the money was all about. I'll never forget the first time I got paid for construction work. I got twenty dollars a

day for myself, and I got paid six twenty dollar bills. I
hardly knew what to do with all that. I put it in one
pocket, then put it in another pocket, then I took it
out again, then . . .

Yes, so anyway, the bank, the Municipal Bank, it
was a Newfoundland Savings thing on Duckworth
Street. I went down there and I put three twenty
dollars in the bank right away. I paid my gas bill and
my board out of the other three twenties. I thought
that was all. Six days later, I get another six twenties.
So that's the way it went. I started saving right away. I
never looked back; I never took any out. I always put
it in. So that's where we went. Then as the family grew
older we formed the company called O'Brien Brothers and a salt fish business in Witless Bay. Between the
middle 1940s and middle 1950s we bought salt fish
from the fishermen. We had a wholesale and retail
store over there and we started supplying. We became
merchants ourselves. Then we went in as three brothers and things got a little bit tougher. It was hard for
three of us to get wages out of it. I split off and went
into trucking business myself. My other two brothers
stayed at it and the fresh frozen fish started coming
along then. I went to Boston with my brother Frank
and we found a person who was interested in invest-
ing some money in the freezing plant in Witless Bay.

I'd say it was seventy dollars return trip on the *Nova
Scotia* from St. John's to Boston. It was fruitful, no
doubt about that. So that's where we went. We split to
avoid trouble, one of the original owners of our fish
plant, his share and he went as manager with another
company. He didn't stay there very long; he started
his own business in Bay Bulls with his own family. He's
the oldest of the family; he's seventy-four or seventy-
five years old. I ran the quick freeze part of it. I had a
brother; he started another business in the fishery.

It kept the family together. I worked hard on
keeping the family together because it was important

not to fall out about anything, business especially. So I would keep them jolly, go kiss them. Above anything else, I'll never fall out with you and not talk to one another. So we visited one another all the time.

We had no children

We had no children. We adopted my wife's sister's child. Her mother died at birth and we took her when she was two weeks old. We also reared her brother. It would be common practice when the mother would go to the hospital for the family. A relative would take some of the family. I'd take one, you take two, for the eight or nine days that the woman was in the hospital. So we took one little boy when he was eight years old and he stayed with us until he got married when he was twenty-one. We didn't adopt him, but we did adopt the other little girl because her father wanted it that way.

If a baby got sick it was a front of the stove job

My mother made us drink cod liver oil. If we had a cold on our chest, she made poultices with Minard's liniment. There was some kind of patent medicine, like Buckley's or whatever was on the go, Minard's liniment or something. One of the other things, if you had a bad throat they'd make you inhale mercurochrome with hot water with a towel over your head. You kept your head over a pan of water. Yes, no doubt, those home remedies were good remedies.

If a baby got sick, it was the front of the stove job for two or three days trying to keep the baby warm and comfortable. You'd stay up all night and shift the cot from one side to the other side and put lots of blankets on the chesterfield or daybed. That was home remedies, and keep you in till your cough was better. Remember, we had no heat, we only had the kitchen stove. Father would probably stay up all night, and mother would take on the day shift.

No, keep yourself warm and dry, and wool clothes kept us all surviving, wool socks and mittens. They would put you to bed and make you soup, things like that. They'd give you some nourishment till you got better.

Neighbours were starving to death on this six cents a day dole thing

Some of the neighbours were better off than we were and some of the fishermen. But some were very poor. We'd eat more brown flour, brown bread, during the Depression and a lot of the people who were on the dole ate it. My mother had a good heart. There were people couldn't eat this brown bread—we could, so she made us eat it. So she would give them our white bread or white flour for their brown flour, within reason. Neighbours were starving to death on this six cents a day dole thing; they were restricted to only brown flour and five or six stable items. That's all, and they just couldn't eat it. So they would come to my mother and she would say you give me ten pounds of brown flour and I'll give you ten pounds of white flour, or whatever it was.

To me it was starvation

There was a lot of people in this community who died with tuberculosis. To me it was starvation. I have no doubt in my mind what killed them at all. They used the word tuberculosis, which was wrong. I can see them now. I was seven, eight, ten years old. I see them little white coffins coming out of the houses with children, for being very sick for six months, a year, and die. Or families like that. Whole families, starvation I think it was, and pride. They wouldn't go look for help.

Didn't know that much about it, because it wasn't contagious, no. The only one I remember was contagious; someone had Scarlet Fever one time. My neighbour, they put up a sign. You weren't allowed to go into the house. People couldn't handle the situation, you got down, you couldn't get up.

I'm living on borrowed time

I had a bypass done in 1980, since then four bypasses done. I had a heart attack in 1989 and I had two since then. I ended up with congestive heart failure. I'm living on borrowed time. I'm out of the hospital now fourteen months. When I was discharged fourteen months ago, they told me I'd be back and forth to the hospital for the rest of my life. I do my medication thing and go to my general practitioner and my specialist every month.

I think the treatment is excellent. As I said my father died when he was fifty-nine years old with the same complaint. There was no such thing as any remedies. There was no heart surgery. I think open heart surgery is a great thing; it has kept me alive.

I think our concerns would be the cut down on hospitals and on health care. You take the Health Science, it has a big backlog of open heart surgery. If you have angina and you have pains, you are ready to go to the hospital and willing to have open heart surgery. You can't get there because of the backlog. That's a concern with anyone over fifty years old. I strongly recommend surgery for that kind of a problem because I went through this myself. I suffered a lot with angina pains before I finally gave up and go and have surgery. And I think it's great; I'd recommend it to anyone. As a matter of fact, I encourage people to go and have it done. You can't live without it.

It's really a concern when you're waiting and you're bumped and bumped by emergencies. Anyone that I see with a heart problem and they are willing to talk, I say have surgery. Before they're not willing to talk, but after, they are. They will, say, "I feel lousy."

I cut my finger sharpening the scythe

As a matter of fact, I cut my finger sharpening the scythe, I've got the mark here. I was by myself, so I went down the road next to the garden. There was an old lady there and she got the knife and went out into the woods. There, with big trees, she said dab your finger right in that. She would break the little bubble and she wrapped it up with cloth that she sterilized herself on the stove. She burnt it herself and she put it on it. There was no such thing as gauze, the tail of a night shirt or something like that. She put it on the stove, kind of browned it, shook it off and put it on the turpentine.

III "You Did What You're Told:" Looking After One's Health

*T*he values of our Newfoundland elders, revealed in the previous chapter, underscore their sense of place, self-sufficiency, resourcefulness and acceptance of what life offers. Much of this was coupled with acceptance of and attention to moral-religious teachings among both Protestants and Catholics. In this chapter we look at ways of maintaining health such as hygiene, exercise, diet, family and community support, and related matters. We ask whether the values we are considering, above all resourcefulness, self-discipline and prudence, underpinned outport Newfoundlanders' approach to healthy living.

For many Newfoundlanders, health and morality were closely intertwined. Hence, a spotless kitchen and long line of clean clothes signalled the "decent" woman labouring for her family and personal honour. This fitted the ideal image of a woman promoted by Irish Catholic and Anglican clergy alike. Likewise, personal hygiene, especially in preparation for Sunday services and Mass, was part of meeting and honouring God. Equally, "rough" food—the fruits of one's own physical-moral labours—was in tune with healthy living, and, for some people the most proper nourishment for God's earthly vessel, the human body. All this, as well as specific church teachings about morality and health, encouraged attention to maxims such as to avoid getting one's feet wet and catching chills, as well as wearing warm clothing, even red flannel underwear. ("You're likely to get sick if you don't listen.") In other words, even in times of changing medical ideas and practices, it was prudent to pay attention to old wisdom; moreover, one should avoid the condemnation of neighbours that one was careless or immoral. Those, for instance, who contracted tuberculosis because of alleged carelessness or poverty might well be stigmatized. It must be said that prudence did not extend to all health matters; for example, there seems to have been little general appreciation of the long-term value of personal dental care.

It is possible to read a moral imperative into many areas of health care, though this depends on each individual. Certainly, informants recalled tonics generally as *medicines*, although the so-called blood purification property of tonics might be seen as both physical and spiritual. Some preventive measures could well have moral overtones; others, such as keeping a dried potato in the pocket to prevent rheumatism, seemed to be exclusively magical.

Many other issues are raised in this chapter. Our female informants, for example, in commenting on "women's matters," mostly express strong conservative Irish Catholic and Anglican beliefs. Accordingly, women's conduct and bodily changes are shrouded in secrecy and mystery, both figuratively and literally. Such secrecy served various social functions, which we note later through the narratives.

The narratives excerpted here constantly remind us that community resources for help and support were especially important. We see that people relied upon their neighbours in ways that are less familiar to many who live in households in urbanized social settings. The comment of one informant seems to express the setting in a particular way: "In growing up, we didn't even know the meaning of stress. We must have had it, but nobody told us we had it."

"What's good for you"

The first four sections in this chapter cover widely held, long-standing health maxims found in books such as J.R.

Black's *The Ten Laws of Health, or How Disease is Produced and Can be Prevented* (1872), copies of which reached Newfoundland. This is just one expression of enduring attention given to hygiene, environmental factors, diet and moral behaviour. General rules were woven with clear-cut "don'ts," like "Don't get your feet wet" and "Don't sit in drafts." Naturally, it is difficult to say how often such maxims were followed. However, the fact that home medicine books and other popular writings stressed such topics suggest that such sayings were commonly forgotten.

Our informants gave us a clear sense that there was generally little discussion, even in schools, on health matters prior to the 1950s. Further, "whether the people listened to it, it's hard to say." Just what advice individuals remembered from childhood, school, formal religious instruction and organizations such as the Anglican Church Lad's Brigade varies considerably. "The only thing is we were told to eat our meals. We had to drink milk and eat what we could afford. That's the only thing I remember." A few people living in St. John's, and who remained at school until senior associate level, recollect a school health book.

New and old ideas often came together in ways that led some people to rather idiosyncratic interpretations of certain "dangers to health." For instance, the germ theory of disease was widely accepted from the 1880s onward and quickly changed many existing beliefs; however, some people held on to environmental ideas. Indeed, it must not be assumed that well-remembered quarantine measures for scarlet fever and other infectious diseases were viewed as keeping away specific bacteria or other organisms. Ideas of contagious particles of dust and of bad air continued to exist. At the same time, fear of contracting such diseases as scarlet fever and tuberculosis was a significant factor in the acceptance of new public health teachings.

A key issue in Newfoundlanders' health during the first half of the twentieth century was nutrition. One informant comments, "the biggest thing was food." Historians, nutritionists and others have often pointed to economic hardships that resulted in inadequate diets. Although some informants indicate that nutritionally all was not well, they remember times of difficulty and shortage, especially "the hungry month of March." The majority say that few had to go short of food for any significant time. "We didn't have an over amount of anything. We were clothed and fed properly and that was it!" There is also recognition that the Newfoundland diet was nutritious. There were certain things that were "good for you," milk, carrots, turnip tops and dandelion greens, for instance, as was "rough, not junk food."

The elders recollect resourcefulness and self-sufficiency, and respond to questions about food in this context. They are not describing their food solely in terms of quality of items purchased, say from the supermarket, as is common today. There is a feeling that home-grown and home-cooked foods—"good plain food"—are superior to canned or other convenience foods. Overall, food is remembered very much as a family affair. What the family grew in the garden and mother cooked in the kitchen are still valued today. This was brought out even more by references to luxuries such as the purchase of fresh fruit at Christmas time.

Although most informants have positive memories of adequate nutrition, others offer unhappy memories. The generally positive opinion stands in contrast with the story told by physician Leonard Miller. Prior to attending a medical conference in mainland Canada in 1950, he was warned by a local doctor's wife not to be another Newfoundlander who said that the island was starving.

●

We have taken the following selections from a good representation of men and women, though there are more women's voices. In this and the following chapter we have excerpted short quotations in order to allow our informants to illustrate our themes of health care in Newfoundland communities.

They didn't have to exercise

Mr. Fergus Babcock, b.1911 , St. Mary's Bay
People years ago did so much walking that they didn't have to exercise, and they worked too hard. You walked a lot. Everywhere you went you had to walk, if you didn't have a horse or a carriage. They had lots of exercise, not many people had cars then, so they walked. If they wanted to go anywhere, they walked.

Mrs. Annette Yetman, b. 1917, Conception Bay
We had plenty of exercise that way, and fresh air. We loved walking then. It was only lately I had to give up walking. I used to walk into my sister's and she would come up here once or twice a week.

"You're liable to get sick if you don't listen"

Mrs. Phyllis Hawkins, b. 1910, Conception Bay
The most they told us about avoiding TB was not to go in the water and get our feet wet. You weren't allowed to take off the shoes and stockings and go in the water if the wind was northeast, that kind of a way. I don't know if they did or not, but Dad used to say, "You're liable to get sick if you don't listen."

My father was very particular when I was a child

Sr. Teresina Bruce, b. 1902, Codroy Valley
I remember my father was very particular when I was a child. I was not to visit these places. I remember saying, "I'm not afraid." He'd say, "No, you're not afraid of TB but you want to bring it home to the rest of us and to the children?" He was very particular about that. Although they were my cousins, I was not allowed to visit. He visited and my mother would visit them, but the young people were not to visit them because it was too dangerous. I don't think anyone ever contracted TB from them.

Youngsters use more toothpaste in a day than I used all my life

Mr. Warren Brazil, b. 1911, St. John's
I don't think people were as conscious of dental care in those days as they are now because the advertising of the product, like Scope or Colgate fluoride toothpaste, you're lambasted with that on the television, so people are more conscious of the health care and the beauty care of teeth than they were in those days.

Mrs. Alice Harris, b. 1920, St. John's
I never had a toothbrush in my life, not when we were young. You know nothing about toothpaste, not in our day because you could not afford it. Today, youngsters use more toothpaste in a day than I used all my life.

Cleanliness was important

Mr. David Strong, b. 1917, St. John's
In hygiene, of course, we were taught that it was important to brush your teeth and bathe regularly, keep your hair clean and eat proper foods.

Sr. Teresina Bruce, b. 1902, Codroy Valley
Cleanliness was important. I remember my mother being very particular, too, if we had a cold—burning handkerchiefs and tissues and whatever we used. Most people washed their hair and kept it cut. I don't remember any special care. Just cleanliness and fresh air. Lots of fresh air in the summertime.

Mrs. Marion Pittman, b. 1925, St. John's
I think fresh air does you good. I don't know how they dealt with it. I know we used to keep the windows opened up at home.

Mrs. Geraldine Reddy, b. 1903, Placentia Bay
We were bathed two or three times a week, that kept us healthy. And washing the hair, my mother used to

rub hot olive oil in it. That was to keep your hair growing and keep it clean and prevent dandruff.

Mr. Brendan Casey, b. 1922, Bonavista Bay
They were very strict, you had to make sure you washed your hands and your face and your ears before you'd go to school. They wanted you to show your best side and keep up with what's the present day.

Sr. Catherine Daly, b. 1899, Placentia Bay
Sometimes you'd come across someone in school that wasn't so well looked after. Indeed, it would be a concern, especially in those days. You didn't have single desks; it depended on who you were next to, and whose mother wasn't so careful about the hair. No, we weren't reluctant to talk about it because everybody knew it. Not alone in the desks, but if you were mixing out around, he or she, I remember one distinctly.

Fine comb, that's all I know. I would imagine the teacher would have something to say to the parents, but I don't know how it was managed. I don't remember any medication for it. That's the only thing I know of. Perhaps the hair would be cut shorter or something like that.

Mrs. Marion Pittman, b. 1925, St. John's
A fine tooth comb was always in the cabinet. You could run it through your hair, afraid you would get anything. But you could pick it up and you know how quick you can form little nits around your head and everything. I was sitting alongside of a girl and she had red hair. I wouldn't tell her, but I went home and told my mother what I see. She phoned the nuns to check on the young girl and sit me somewhere else.

Rough food, just ordinary rough food

A lot of people thought years ago that it was terrible in Newfoundland, but it wasn't. Everybody had their fields, they had their cows, and they had their fresh butter, they had their eggs and you had excess eggs to sell and barter for something else in the stores, food supplies or whatever you might want. There wasn't much cash because at that time, the way the system was, the merchant would give out—a fitout they used to call it years ago—give out so much provisions you needed, if you were going fishing. And you paid when you sold your fish. The fish was all salted and dried, which is a very long procedure, then shipped away in the fall to foreign countries. So you didn't get paid for your fish until you sold it to the merchant in the fall.

Then you had your eggs, your hens, and you had sheep—so you had lambs—and your cows were calving and you had the females usually. They would kill in the fall, in November, and the meat would be cut up for the barrels, and covered with snow and when you wanted it you went out. You had no cold storage or anything, nothing in electricity, no freezers or anything.

My father and my older brother were hunters, so they could hunt partridge and sell them at the time. Granted, a partridge was only twenty-five cents. This was before the war started in '39. I was keeping house then, and that's what it was, fifty cents a brace.

What was good about it, too, people shared. If you had a cow milking, there'd be people come with bottles for milk. I can remember before I left school, the first thing mother would do in the morning, she would strain the milk, the fresh milk. There would be a crock ready for me when I'd be going to school, because father would milk the cow when he come in from fishing, seven o'clock. Then you'd strain that milk, and that's a drawn out procedure too because it would have to stay until the evening and then the cream thickens up on it, then you scald it the next morning. What you got this morning, you scalded in the evening. Then you let it get cool and you made your butter.

Mrs. Julia Collins, b. 1921, Southern Shore
There wasn't much you could buy, even at stores when I was really young. Just the basic foods they would have there. They would have nothing in the form of glasses or dishware or anything like that. It would be mostly food and then they'd have lumber for caskets, and the caskets would be made, and the material to cover them and the handles. You had to buy it in the store there, because the roads were blocked. So that was bought then, even the sheeting tools, just linen, to wrap around the body in the casket. That would be bought.

There was plenty to eat

Sr. Teresina Bruce, b. 1902, Codroy Valley
There was plenty to eat, good food, because we had our own vegetables and my father went fishing in the summer and they caught all kinds of fish which they cured for the winter. It was difficult to buy fresh fruit but there were people in the Codroy Valley who grew apples and plums if you lived in places near the river. We didn't grow them. We were too near the sea. You could buy fresh fruit and you could pick strawberries and bakeapples and all kinds of small fruit. We had plenty of these and we'd preserve these for the winter.

My mother was a good cook. Most of the women were good cooks in those days and they knew how to make the best of what they had. That was important. We didn't have luxuries. We didn't have fresh fruit except at Christmas time or perhaps in the summertime when you could get it easily. We had our own lambs and our own cattle, our own chickens, hens, and our own eggs. All these things were good food. Good plain food.

It wasn't polluted in any way

Mr. Billie-Mike Rossiter, b. 1927, Southern Shore
I never saw store bread or baker's bread until I left home. Everybody baked their own bread and, as I said, my mother was an excellent cook and she baked ordinary bread. She also baked what the Irish, I think, called soda bread made with buttermilk and soda. That was extra special and she did the buns and cookies and that sort of thing. We had very good food and so had most of our neighbours. We went back and forth to our neighbour's houses and I think everyone lived at about the same rate. Everybody did their own cooking, baking and preserving. The food was certainly fresh. It wasn't polluted in any way.

Porridge for our breakfast and . . . cod liver oil

Mr. Albert Boland, b. 1921, Southern Shore
I remember some times before we went to school, we'd have to have porridge for our breakfast with nutmeg on it. We always had to have porridge, and after we had our porridge we had to have cod liver oil. Cod liver oil went after the porridge. This started off our meal day.

My father worked at the fish wharf down at Crosbie's before he went away and he made a good living at that. He was a fish inspector. So we always had plenty to eat, just the regular food like, Sunday, cooked dinners and Tuesdays would be soup, and Wednesday would be fish day, and Thursday would be dinner cooked again, and Friday would be fish again. So these are the meals that we'd always eat. We had lots of herring and fish.

We had plenty of berries

Mrs. Roberta Haynes, b. 1921, Labrador
We had plenty of berries that we picked in the summer; we used to have four barrels of partridge berries for the winter and have a barrel, a big keg of bakeapples, and, besides, we'd have some bottled up, and we'd have lots of fish. And in the fall there was no merchant in the head of St. Michael's Bay, so Dad, when he was fishing, he'd go to the merchant up in the fishing ships harbour and he'd buy the rough food, enough to last the winter.

Flour, butter, molasses, beef and pork, things like that. Milk, soda biscuits, and things. We never had a lot of sweet candy; we used to make our own candy. Make molasses candy, and boil sugar and colour it with berry juice and cocoa, and when it was cold we'd cut it all up, and it tasted as good as the candy you buy at the store today.

Pork and cabbage . . .

Mrs. Betty Corcoran, b. 1925, Southern Shore
Whatever was put to the table we had to eat it. Pork and cabbage, and greens and soup, hearty meals. Well, they, the women, had to work out in the gardens like me when I got married; my husband was one half fisherman and one half farmer, so we used to go in the gardens all the time and set the vegetables and weed them. We worked hard, I must say. That was my exercise.

You had to eat that before you went to school

Mostly in the morning you had to have porridge or cream of wheat. You had to eat that before you went to school. That's good for you. But the overall diet really wasn't good for us. It wasn't said you should eat lettuce, you should eat tomatoes. If it was there and if you liked it you ate it, and if you didn't like it, you didn't eat it. There was no emphasis put on what you should eat because it was good for you.

I think the more we get nutrition and health education, the more money we're going to save on health care. If you eat the proper foods, you're going to have a better lifestyle, you won't have health problems. So the money that's spent on education is probably paying off ten times. You're not going to spend time on cures. It is really a preventative.

Now there were people who didn't live well

Mrs. Julia Collins, b. 1921, Southern Shore
Now, there were people who didn't live well, because you didn't have this start, you didn't have cattle and you didn't have lots of things. There's some people, not that they're not energetic, sometimes they get so poor that they kind of lose interest. Because, I remember Frank telling me one time about a family here, and they had a big family and they used to grow a lot of vegetables, and his father would always save a bag of seed; the smaller potatoes were picked out for seed, you'd cut them and they'd sprout, and he would give them to the man but they'd be so hungry that they'd eat them when they'd get them, instead of planting them.

They had no money to buy anything. He had a big family. There are people here have seventeen children, the biggest kind of families.

Tonics

Whatever recollections exist about nutrition in the past, Newfoundlanders, like many people elsewhere up until the fifties, often felt the need of the "old-fashioned" tonic. Beliefs about the value of tonics usually focused on the need for purification, especially of the blood. This concept was already losing ground in regular medicine as our informants were growing up.

Particularly well known were spring tonics. Administered

at the tail end of winter, usually towards the end of March, these served as preventatives, treatment, or even a "body overhaul." Indeed, our informants made clear that spring tonics amounted to almost a community wide practice. A striking range of substances was used. These varied from commonplace "traditional" bitters and the well-known wild cherry—not to mention the Newfoundland favourite, cod liver oil—to the less frequent brandy and eggs. Many of our informants still take "tonics"; however, they are associated more with vitamins than with the notion of cleansing.

You weren't very active in the winter

Mr. Paddy Nolan, b. 1919, Southern Shore
Well, the old people had funny ideas. Mostly in the spring of the year, they'd clean the blood, mostly with the youngsters. That's what their idea was. Maybe they were right. You weren't very active in the winter. In storms you were in the house for days. The schools were closed. I remember the old man going up on the horse and if there was a storm up, picking up all the children and bringing them home in the horse and slide. Going to school, you'd have to walk to the head of the village, about a mile, with a junk of wood under your arm.

More so in the springtime than any other time, you would get sick so quick they believed

Mrs. Roberta Haynes, b. 1921, Labrador
They used to go to work and steep out spruce boughs, get spruce boughs, clean boughs, and wash them and steep them out and then drain off the water, the liquor, and put it in bottles and take a drink. It would give you a good appetite, and the dogwood rind would clean your blood, and things like this we would do. In the morning you were supposed to take the dogwood.

The same way you were supposed to take a spoonful of cod liver oil in the morning, to keep your lungs

healthy, they used to tell us. We'd take it every day,
most whatever coming out of our spring, that's when
Dad and Mom believed you could get run down and
get sick. You'd take a drink once a day, a glassful.
More so in the springtime than any other time. You
wouldn't get sick so quick, they believed.

A small glass of Epsom salts

I remember distinctly that in the spring of the year,
my father, you'd see him going with this bottle,
Epsom salts mixed in a bottle, and you'd have to take
every morning a small glass of Epsom salts, and a
spoonful of sulphur to clean your blood. But we were
always pretty healthy. Of course, we had everything
that we could have on the go; we had mumps and
whooping cough, and, of course, we had itch. Everything on the go, we got it.

If you were dropping down

Mrs. Mary Whelan, b. 1902, Conception Bay
We'd often drink a spring tonic of milk and eggs. Beat
up your egg and put some milk in it. That was a spring
tonic in them days if you were dropping down. You
want to take more than one. You'd take one every day.
That's really tonic, built up your strength. And Brick's
Tasteless cod liver oil which you can't get today. That
was a spring tonic. And Beef Iron Wine is something,
I don't think you can get that today.

I remember there was a tonic used mostly in the spring

Sr. Catherine Daly, b. 1899, Placentia Bay
I remember there was a tonic used mostly in the
spring. It was a bought tonic, although some of the
Sisters in their early days would have, of course, senna
tea. We didn't have it, but Wampoles cod liver oil, I
remember taking that, especially if you had a cold.
And you had a lot of fish.

I heard some of the sisters saying their parents

used to give them senna tea to purify the blood, but I don't remember taking anything. We did take Wampoles for a tonic if you're run down a bit or if you got too many colds, but it was mostly in the spring tonic. Or a cough mixture that you would buy on the shelf.

In the spring your blood is run down, I don't know what purifying it meant, but that's what it was taken for I think. I don't know what we took. I remember taking the tonic. We'd be run down after the winter, hard winters in those days.

There was sort of a feeling that these things would get rid of the poisons built up in your system

Sr. Teresina Bruce, b. 1902, Codroy Valley
I remember one of the things. If you had fever, if your temperature was up and you were hot, the important thing was to give you a laxative. With children it was what you call senna tea. I had to take it. Dreadful stuff. If you were older, it was Epsom salts or castor oil. There was some sort of a feeling that these things would get rid of the poisons built up in your system. If you had a bad cold that wasn't getting any better you might get some kind of a cherry bark and you'd steep that. It wasn't real cherries but that's what the people called it. It was some kind of bark of a tree that you steeped and they gave you that for a cold. It also was supposed to give you an appetite because it tasted rather bitter and I suppose the bitterness helped. There were a lot of home made things but that was one home made remedy that I remember.

Mrs. Alice Harris, b. 1920, St. John's
Oh, yes, sulphur and molasses. It seemed like, after the winter they said, you'd lose all your energy and Mom always said that it cleaned your blood out. "You won't get pimples or anything like that if you take this." You'd take it for at least a couple of weeks. Every morning you would have this sulphur and molasses. And everyone in the house would take it. There were

lots of others. Beef Iron Wine, and they say brandy and eggs is a good tonic. If you're not feeling well, if your nerves are down, take that for a couple of mornings and that's good. Raw eggs in brandy.

Family and community support

It is widely recognized that the well being and health of individuals and their communities are linked in many subtle ways. This is aside from long standing and conspicuous public policies that dictate many services affecting public health, such as safe water supplies and vaccinations. Current "prescriptions" for a healthy community include support services at various levels. In fact, in Newfoundland, outport families, unified by Christian denominational identities and moral expectations, have long been a first recourse and resource in time of need. This, too, was built on reciprocal partnerships facilitated by extended families. Women, for instance, would share their household surplus to help other women and their families through the rough spots. Needs were often communicated through informal gossip or subtle breaks in the daily rhythm in the community. They were recognized by unusual activity, or a lamp light on in another home late at night. This drew attention, curiosity, involvement and offers of aid whether openly solicited or not. The experience of sharing the struggle fostered friendship and relationships. "Everyone was called 'uncle' then," and that lasted throughout the lives of household members.

People reinforced their help in practical ways by organizing church and other voluntary associations within the community. Collections in aid of those in need or in crisis were carried out to meet the occasion. People prayed in times of crisis and armed themselves with ritual-spiritual objects such as medals or scapulars; the rosary was offered up daily in Catholic households.

As we read below about the family and community support, we note that the elders remember it largely in connection with pregnancies, illnesses and so on. Yet, they make clear it extended in many other ways.

Mr. Paddy Nolan, b. 1919, Southern Shore
The community was closer. The church and the church hall were the centre of the community. The church controlled your life then, more or less. It was all built around the church.

We were all as one

Mrs. Mary Whelan, b. 1902, Conception Bay
When someone had a problem or took ill, you'd go to a neighbour to get advice to know what to do, especially if you had youngsters. Where we lived, we had great neighbours.

Neighbours, if you or anyone had anything the matter with them in the whole town, everyone would know it. For example, when I got married and went to Daniel's Cove, there was a woman there with a family. They weren't the best off—often I'd take a piece of beef out of my barrel and run it across the road to her for her dinner. I often done that. But no one would know that, only me and her, not even my own husband would know that. Not that he'd care, but like the scripture says, "Don't let the left hand know what the right hand does." Don't talk about all your good deeds. Leave that for the Lord.

The way it is in the communities, if there's anything the matter with you, it's known all over. In those small communities it's all "one will help the other." If you sees someone's light on late in the night, you know there's something wrong. Well, the first thing in the morning, you'll try to find out why she had her light on. That's the way it was in the community we were in. We were all as one.

I often took butter and sugar and went to another woman's house because I knew her circumstances. Her son comes here to visit me now, she's dead. He comes to visit me and he'll often say, "Many's a time we'd be without sugar only for you."

Guaranteed the neighbours would come by to help out

Mr. James Keilly, b. 1923, St. John's
If there was somebody sick on the street where you
were living, guaranteed, neighbours would come by
to help out, whether it was to cook a meal or clean up.
I remember one time, my mother was after having
one of her babies at home, and she had phlebitis in
her legs and at the same time we came down with the
mumps. We were all very young then and one of our
neighbours, she'd take all of us down Saturdays to her
house and give us our bath. And if there was anything
she could do with regards to helping out around the
house, she did the same.

And then, when Mom was expecting one of her
children, she would always have what she would call a
"maid" come in for one month to look after us, and
just to be there, I suppose. Mom would pay $5.00 a
month, and that was wonderful at that time. That was
great then. Plus she lived in with us. I can remember
some of the girls now that we had, and people would
laugh at that today, but it's the truth just the same.

We were all together, we helped each other like
that, in sickness and if anyone got sick, we'd go and
help them. I remember we used to go to bring water.
They would have no water then, or service. And we'd
make splits and bring in their coal for them. We were
supposed to go and shovel snow for anybody that
couldn't get out, and go on messages for them.

People were concerned about each other

Mr. Abe Davis, b. 1913, Conception Bay
People were concerned about each other. Like, if
anyone took sick and they had vegetables in the
ground, they didn't have to worry about getting their
vegetables out. You'd collect a bunch of people, you
go and dig the potatoes, pick them up and bring them
out. If they had hay to make, same thing. If the man
was sick, someone went and did what had to be done,

their house to paint or whatever. You'd pitch in, that was the thing to do. They would do the same for you. And you'd be insulting to ask how they charged.

The communities now, there are so many people moved in those communities. They have sort of mixed into that same style of thing they came from. They came from, say, Hermitage or Fortune Bay, and those places. Now they came and they mixed into communities that there's nothing at all like they had left, so they couldn't mix in with the people 'cause they didn't know anybody. Like you go to church in the morning and there's 150 people in church, you're lucky if you know 25 or 30 of them by name. You avoid that person because you don't know them.

Women's health: clothing and silence

In contrast to the family and community support just considered, women's matters—be they viewed as a "problem" or the normal life-cycle changes—received little overt community support. Indeed, one striking feature of Newfoundland gender relationships conveyed by our informants is the apparent restraint, silence and shame that surrounds sexuality and fertility. These are remembered as topics only for married women. As with most matters sexual, "everything was hush-hush" and children, especially, were excluded. Nowadays, many informants wonder how the current openness has come about. They recognize, even if they are not impressed, the current arguments that normal sexuality is part of being "healthy." But this prompts the question, What is normal?

As our elderly Newfoundlanders were growing up, they did not see sexuality as a health or medical issue; they saw it as one of morals, as many still do. It was very much part of everyone's value system, of self-discipline, but especially for women. Even when sexuality became a medical problem and required doctor's attention, the strong attitudes of the church regarding sexuality were apparent. Many informants may not be comfortable with the openness of today, but they appreciate the more readily available advice from the new expertise of psychologists, psychiatrists and marriage counsellors.

This earlier emphasis on silence and discretion about sexual matters illustrates some of the controls western society has placed on sexuality. These controls are often "explained" as the result of the power of the church through its doctrines and teachings. The discretion and silence about sexuality and fertility evident in the information presented here were part of the social discipline, perhaps to check the potentially socially disruptive attraction of sexual expression for pleasure and channel and limit the reproductive power of women to family and household.

We have not organized the information on life changes in this section under specific topics. In fact, our informants offered comments less readily than on other matters. Protestant informants were more reluctant to talk about sexuality and fertility than Catholics. However, we cannot say whether a greater degree of silence existed in Protestant communities. In general, repetitiveness in the observations that follow emphasizes the sexual silence and the value placed on self-discipline that went with it. This value is generally retained, although many elders accept the greater openness of today.

Formal sex education was nonexistent for our informants. The clergy were known to offer advice, though this was more about the dangers of prolonged courtship or to stress the marital "duties" of women. Young people generally learned about sexual matters from peers; as one woman stated, "We learned from one another." Some informants suggested that boys exchanged information more readily.

A young woman's first menstrual period was sometimes accompanied by oblique advice from the mother, which may have done little to alleviate the anxiety. Others received no parental help. A typical comment was: "Mother didn't tell us about periods. You just heard it from friends." In fact, the main source of reassurance for girls was the fact that their friends were having similar experiences. Information exchanged about menstruation included methods of alleviating pain, such as applying warmth (e.g., from an "old hot plate put in the oven") and using "painkillers" like "222" or aspirin. Parents commonly used clothing and silence to conceal pregnancy from their children. Discussion was avoided in front of children, and parents made them leave the room when a pregnant woman entered. "It was never mentioned. Funny about that, isn't it? You weren't allowed to say nothing like that anyway, you couldn't ask nothing like that. Oh, we came up from under a rock or the stork brought us."

Communities rarely offered open support to someone who was pregnant outside marriage. It was an embarrassing and shameful matter that triggered painful gossip about the woman and her family. Sometimes such a pregnancy was concealed by organizing a quick marriage; the church adopted a hostile attitude to such pregnancies, and "marriages of convenience" were conducted reluctantly.

Knowledge about contraception was provided more by peers than by family. Boys and girls learned about such unreliable preventive methods as "hauling out." "We didn't know what a French safe was until we got out on the streets," but condoms were nevertheless not generally available, and no evidence has been found of Newfoundlanders making their own from, say, animal intestines. Belief that breast feeding served as a contraceptive seems to have been widespread.

The opinion that some couples "probably never wanted half of them" should not be casually dismissed, for each new pregnancy and childbirth brought additional risks, burdens and uncertainties. The incidence of deliberate abortion is difficult to assess, but was probably not high. Some informants don't think it really happened, though others remember knitting needles and "some doctors willing to perform abortion." Infanticide was probably not common, though it did exist. Rather than this or abortion, adoption of children born outside marriage was common. Grandparents or other close relatives often adopted children informally; formal adoptions were rare.

Recollections about menopause are also limited. Many of

the women would agree with the comment "you might hear about it once in a while, but very seldom."

The mission fathers told us what to do

Mrs. Mildred Meaney, b. 1923, Placentia Bay
This is a long story: The mission fathers, the priests, were the ones that told you what to do and how to do it, and you went to the priest and you told him. It was a mortal sin to deny your husband his marital rights, so she had to go tell that. "Father, I denied John his marital rights four times last month." The Father said, "My dear, you know you can't do that."

This mission father, he had a night for the married people, and a night for the single boys and a night for the single girls. I was thirteen and I was allowed to go. Here was this big old priest with this Roman collar on and a big pair of beads hanging down—all that's just to intimidate you—and he said, "My sermon today is going to be on courtship and marriage." He said, "I understand that there's a lot of couples around here going together longer than six months. If you're going together six months, get married."

He said he understands, they were after telling him in confession and he said another thing: "This long kissing is a temptation, it's a mortal sin, give it up." So that day, on our way home we passed a couple that weren't very intelligent, but they had been going together a couple of years, so the crowd went up to this woman and said, "Now, Ag, remember what the priest said, that this long kissing is a mortal sin." She said, "Look, Pat could kiss for a week and it wouldn't be a venial sin."

The church planned your family, a woman couldn't plan it, she couldn't deny her husband his marital rights without committing a mortal sin and they're still talking that bull today. I picked up a woman on the road one time, an older woman, she was down to visit her daughter and she said, "I've had fourteen children and I wish I were young and could have fourteen more." That's how she felt about it, but every woman didn't feel like that. People had big families. Twelve and thirteen children to a family; there was something wrong with the man or the woman if they only had four or five.

Never used to speak about it

Never used to speak about it. The babies were always brought by the stork or some old lady came and brought the baby. They didn't know the scientific part of it at that time. There was nothing talked about in the sexual sense to children. They do now though, and I think it's better for the children. Yes, at a certain age I think it's better for them to learn, but not too young, they don't know, they wouldn't understand it. That's what I think sometimes, that they know too much, but some children, it don't make a difference in them, they'll go ahead anyway. It's hard to say.

Baby aboard

Now you go to the doctor for everything, women, as soon as she finds out she's pregnant, she visits the doctor and goes four or five times between that and delivery, they go through a race course of treatment, the doctor follows it all.

One time the average woman was hid away when she got pregnant and never let anybody see her. I visited a house in Avondale one day last week. This was a family that was religious but she had this blouse on and an arrow going down here marked Baby Aboard. So the attitudes changed. An old man in Avondale, he used to call them Josey's; he said, "I hates to see a woman with Josey's on her." That was a maternity jacket they used at that time.

The one you christened on Thursday was the caboose

Abortion was never even mentioned. I don't think they took place. There might be miscarriages or something like that, but not deliberate abortions. When Father Houlihan came here, he was out meeting the parishioners, which they never did before, only this last eight or ten years, and he was shaking hands with everyone. The second Sunday he was here, this woman came to him and he said, "Did I christen a baby belonging to you this week?" She said "Yes." He said, "I understand you have eight more children" and she said "Yes." He said, "You're a good Catholic woman, keep up the good work." She said, "I got news for you Father. The one you christened on Thursday was the caboose."

It wasn't talked about very much, the change of life

It wasn't talked about very much, the change of life. Some women when they'd have their last child, probably shortly after they'd be over, something like that. I was over it myself. Sheila was the last child I had, I must have been around thirty-six and everything left me then, I was over it, and I was some glad. I was over my periods, and I was some glad because some people do be miserable on the change of life. Some people has them late and their nerves gives out. But I had no bother. I don't remember about anyone else. I don't think people talked about that much. Perhaps most women know that's something that had to be.

It was almost a shameful thing

Mrs. Mary Whelan, b. 1902, Conception Bay
Pregnancy wouldn't be talked about. In our day if you saw anyone pregnant, they came into your house, your mother is liable to hide you away so you wouldn't see the person who was going to have a baby. Even if they were married, they wouldn't go out and around. It was almost a shameful thing. There was one came

to the house and when I saw her coming I said, "My God, what's the matter with her? Look how big she is." She said, "Go in the room and wait till she goes away." If they weren't married, my God, that was an awful disgrace. You wouldn't know that till it was born.

What a disgrace

That'd be an awful thing when a young girl became pregnant. It's so common now. That was in my mind the other day. I was fourteen or fifteen when my cousin got pregnant. Well, she married him right away, that was the thing to do. What a disgrace, a shock everyone got, and that this girl got. She married in the cove. What a disgrace she was to the family. It was shocking, it was terrible.

They'd be gossiping. That often comes in my mind now. It's so common today, young ones having babies and going on. There was no abortion then. In my growing up, she was the only one in our place to become pregnant like that. The way it is now, it's so common today.

They'd always keep the baby. And, if you'd be living with the parents, her parents looked after it. And they'd think as much about it as they would if it was their own child. The nature was there. I reared a daughter, my daughter's daughter. She calls me "Mom," though she knows the difference. In fact, she got married in my home. She lives here in town, up the street from me. It's not everyone knows it.

I looked after her till she was eighteen years old, through school and everything, and she must have been fifteen or eighteen years old before I told her the difference. When she started to go out, I told her the difference, but in the meantime she knew in her mind somehow, that I wasn't, I was too old to be her mother. It made no difference, it looked like it was instinct. She knew. Now she lives next door to her real

mother and calls her all the time. She calls her by her
first name, like a sister.

Some were always moping around at the change of life

People talked of the menopause. I had a baby on the
change of life. I was forty-eight, that's what I was. You
used to hear, people would be talking, "My, that poor
bugger is pregnant and she's forty-eight."

Some were always moping around at the change of
life, couldn't go here, couldn't go there. I went to a
dance when I was three months on her, me friend
didn't know I was pregnant, went to a dance in Grate's
Cove on St. Stephen's Day and I danced them twenty-
one dances and walked back home the next morning
with me friend. She was born six months after. Me
friend says, "How did you hide it?" I had the same
clothes on I had on all the time, I didn't try to hide it.
I never wore a pair of corsets in me life.

About a week after St. Stephen's Day I was going to
this woman's house just up over the hill, she looked
through the window and when I got in she says, "My
God, is you swelled?" I said, "Yes, six months from
now you'll see the swelling I got."

She says, "You're not?" Everyone was alike there,
what one knew the other knew. I says, "Yes, I'm three
months pregnant." "And you down in Grate's the
other night and danced every dance." I said, "That
only made it a bit loose."

You were scared to death at the first period

Mrs. Marion Pittman, b. 1925, St. John's
You were scared to death at the first period. I was
going to Presentation and all of us together. I remember that day now when you come to that age one
would be coming in "I got it, I got it."

And you had no such thing as a pad or anything,
flannelette cut in strips and you had to clean that and
boil it in Gillett's Lye and blue it and put away for the

next month. You'd never hear tell of a missed period. For one thing, you didn't know if you should take anything.

Over in the drugstore there last year one day I was picking up something and this young man came up and he had Tampax in his hand and he said to the girl "This is regular, haven't you got the other one?" And I looked at him and I said, "Oh, my God." Can you picture it? I couldn't believe it. You know my father; my God, I never heard him swear in the house. There was a saying, "He's like an old dog." But this guy, not too long ago, I said to my neighbour next door what happened, she said "May, that's nothing. They're all doing that now."

Mother would never talk to you

Mother would never talk to you. If she was pregnant and somebody come in, you would go to your bedroom or go out and play. We learned on the street from one another. That's's the way we were. I agree with what they are doing today, really I do, the schools and that. Some of it and some you don't, but this, sure, you didn't know what you were in the world for when you were getting married.

We never knew anything like about pregnancy. That's was private. The world knows it today. Some poor person gets pregnant, anything can happen to any kid, it's only a stupid minute and it's over, her life is ruined and another life coming into the world. I believe in abortion. I'd rather see it aborted.

Usually the girl's mother would take the baby, or else it was passed on to Salvation Army people. The Anchorage was only up on Cook Street, our back door was on Cook Street.

You heard a little bit about abortion because of The Anchorage, but not a great lot. I remember one young girl died, the mother and father were in the bed, she had taken an overdose of something. Years

ago, these things were more or less covered up. Today
everything is out in the open which I think is a good
thing, for it to come out, because it puts a scare in
people. Don't you think so? I would say a good many
older people support abortion. I think I'd rather see
a child aborted than abused for the rest of its life.

When I was a little girl, everything was hush hush

Mrs. Viola Gushue, b. 1930, St. John's
When I was a little girl, everything was hush hush.
And I can remember some of Mom's friends—it's a
funny thing. They'd always have time in the after-
noons for people to go back and forth. And you were
"to be seen and not heard." And if they were talking
about somebody having a baby or anything else, my
dear, you had to get out. You were either out in one
of the other rooms or out in the back yard. Nothing
was discussed.

And even when we were getting older, nothing
discussed. Mom and Dad would never discuss anything like that and Mom and probably her lady
friends. Nothing was discussed. I remember the last
couple of children my mother had. The rest of us were
born at home, but when she was going to the hospital
she would tell us that she was going around the bay for
a new baby. When I think back, it was so foolish, and
now the younger ones are coming home telling the
parents everything.

But when I was a little bit older, she had this baby,
Annie. The war started in 1939. She was born around
1938, the year before the war started. And I knew
then about Mom being pregnant and I mentioned it
to her. And I got such a slap that to this day I still
remember. It was just the way the times were. I don't
blame Mom for it. It's just the way the times were.

I couldn't talk Granny talk

Mrs. Julia Collins, b. 1921, Southern Shore .

When I was expecting my second child—she's thirty-six years old now, she was born in June—I came into Mom's one day and it was really warm. "Well, Julia, why haven't you got your coat on?" I said, "Why, Mom?" "You're so big now." She thought I should have a coat on. I said, "Go away, indeed I'm not wearing no coat, I'll melt." It was really a hot day. That's's just the way.

One day I was down to my grandmother's house and I was sat off in the chair with my leg crossed and she came over and she put my two feet to the floor and she said, "Julia, go cover your modesty." But today, when I told that to my crowd, they laughed their heads off at that. We got to remember, she was born in 1869, so I was a young girl then.

You just heard about it from your friends. That's's where you found out everything. Years later, we said to Mom, "You never talked to us." She said, "I couldn't talk Granny talk." That's's what she said to us. I don't blame her. It was the way she grew up as well.

But today the boys and the girls talk. It's all alike today. It's alright, you know, because it's a part of nature. But at that time, they didn't look at it that way. And there was no talk about family planning. They didn't know. There was no such thing. No, the babies came along and that was it. If you got pregnant, you got pregnant, if you didn't, you didn't. They didn't know what it was then.

The girl's father wouldn't let him go to see her

When grandmother was having my mother, her sister was living in St. John's and she got pregnant. The man was gone away, he used to go to sea. It was in the wintertime and she left a letter at his house; she came home. I think it was around a couple of months or three months before she gave birth. Anyway, she came home and it was wintertime when he got back because in these times they went to the Mediterranean and everywhere else bringing fish and bringing them back, different things, exchange, and so on. So when he got back and got the letter he walked up to Ferryland, about forty miles, to see her and went to the door and told them who he was and that he wanted to see her.

But the old man wouldn't let him go in to see her, the girl's father, wouldn't let him go in to see her. And she spent three months upstairs, she wasn't due right away. So she stayed upstairs and her sister brought up her meals and that type of thing. Anyway she gave birth and she got a girl.

They didn't get married, no, because she went to the States. Her aunt, a spinster, she had no children and she lived quite near them so she took the child and Bess went away to the States. The child stayed here in Newfoundland until she got to be a hardier girl, then she went to the States. Bess married years later. There was always little things like that somebody would be put out about.

If you were a young woman, not married and you became pregnant, it was something that the family would try to hide. There was no way you could hide it because the child had to be born, but I suppose there was a stigma attached to it. She was afraid of the father, see. The old father wouldn't let her go out. Well, she had to come down after but she went to live with aunt Betsy, see. That's was her aunt who lived right next door. Aunt Betsy was living in the old homestead with her mother's parents and her grandmother's parents lived there, they were there in the house. So she reared her anyway and she went to the States and she married after. She never had children of her own. I visited her, Christmas, years ago, her husband was dead then.

They didn't use pads

Mrs. Alice Harris, b. 1920, St. John's
Your mother wouldn't even discuss periods with us.
Young girls would tell you what happened to them
and wonder did it happen to you yet. Then they
didn't use pads, they used flannelette and made their
own and washed them up and cleaned them and kept
them for the next time.

While you're nursing you never came on your period

"Oh no, I'm not having another one," they used to
say, and I'll tell you what they did do though, I heard
my mother say, and I did it myself, "you nursed your
baby for two years." One would be running the floor
and you'd take it up and nurse it and while you're
nursing your baby you never came on your period, so
therefore you wouldn't get pregnant. I know that.
That's was a preventive measure I did myself. You
nursed your baby because you didn't want to bother
with bottles, or things like that. Things were different
than they are now. There was a lot of flies around
years ago, so it was cleaner to nurse your baby than to
be bothered with old bottles. That's's right, everybody will talk about there was two years between each
child. The only thing they would discuss, oh no, I'm
not having another child, but they wouldn't do anything, I don't think, about it.

The change of life

Oh, yes. Like my mother, she went on the change. I
was going on eighteen then. I said "Mother, what's
wrong?" She had her last baby. She used to feel weak,
she'd be walking, next thing she'd be down, feel weak.
I said "Mother what's wrong with you?" And she said,
"I'm on the change of life." That's all I knew this was
happening, so this is what would happen to her, she'd
just walk along the street and faint. She didn't know
what caused it and she didn't do anything about it,

but she just had to be careful. I didn't ask her what the change of life was but I sort of figured it out, talking to friends and their mother and you'd get information. I thought at this time she probably wouldn't have any more children and this was the change in her body.

The priest wouldn't marry you until after night

Mr. Charles Tarrant, b. 1899, Southern Shore
The only thing I heard any name for was when a girl became pregnant. Not so much in the community, but a lot of times in the family. I don't know if it's pride or what, sure, sometimes the family was alright but a lot of time they weren't. Then if you got married, if you had to get married, the priest wouldn't marry you until after night. He was in Ferryland and he wouldn't come up and you'd walk down to his house, yourself and the groom, and he married you and you came home.

A lot of them, when they found out they were pregnant, got married. A lot of times the community didn't know at all. Yes, 'cause they used to say then, you got married and a short time after that you had a baby. And you'd see all the women then counting on their fingers to see how many months.

This was supposed to be the custom before I can remember anything then. I had an old uncle down here, grandfather's brother, and he got a girl in Ferryland in trouble and she was put upstairs, this is the story I used to hear, until the baby was born, and then she was allowed to come down.

I didn't know until she had them

Sr. Teresina Bruce, b. 1902, Codroy Valley
My mother was pregnant, and I was a big girl, I was the oldest and I didn't know she was having a baby. I didn't know until she had them. I said, "Mother, where did you get it?" She said, "The doctor brought

it to me." I looked after her, I was the oldest, and I looked after the children, but I never knew, and when she'd be getting pregnant she wore loose clothes and I never knew she was pregnant. She had all the babies home. Sometimes a midwife, sometimes the doctor. When we were in the States, a doctor came but home here, a woman came.

The midwife born the baby, she would come back. I took some responsibility for looking after mother at that time in caring for her. She stayed in bed for nine days. I would see to her meals, that type of thing. And the midwife would come in every day and look after things. Even if there were clothes there with blood on it, she wouldn't let me see that. I guess the midwife probably cleaned that up for her, but I wasn't allowed to see anything like that as a child. I wasn't supposed to know anything about that.

They used to go in the woods for polly peachum

Mrs. Phyllis Hawkins, b. 1910, Conception Bay
Girls, when they start their periods, sometimes they wouldn't be regular and they used to go in the woods. They used to pick some sort of herb they called polly peachum. They used to steep it, put it on the stove and boil it, and make a liquid out of it. They'd give it to the girls to drink and that would help regulate or clear up any disorders that they may have. If there was nothing else wrong, it would help. A lady down in Kelligrews told me that she had to drink a lot of it when she was young. I never saw it and I don't know what it looks like, and I never had to have it because I was healthy and I never had any trouble. I know my mother used to steep the juniper and the smell of it. I'd go outdoors when it was on. That's's the only thing that I know it was used for.

Never talked in front of us

Mr. Cyril Slaney, b. 1926, St. John's
That's was something that my mother never did,
never talked about in front of us, maturing and
changes in our body, stuff like that. Even if a woman
next door was having a baby, it was never talked about
(that she is going to have a new baby at such and such
a time). We would know something strange was going
on. And we never ever talked about it amongst ourselves. No.

Growing up, never heard anything about abortion

Abortion is not on the go that long. I've never heard
of it, growing up, never heard anything about abortion. It is like homosexuals now, gay people; I never
heard anything like that when we were growing up. It
is only lately. If you said that person is having a "gay"
time, that meant that they were happy, that people
were all gay there, happy-go-lucky. But it has a different meaning now. Like on television the other night,
where this little outport was called "Gaytown" or
something like that, so they are going to have the
name changed. Times have changed.

As far as rape is concerned, we never heard anything about anyone being raped when we were growing up. I suppose because adults didn't talk about
those things in front of children. We knew what was
happening in our neighbourhood, but not so much in
town. Very few people had radios even. In our neighbourhood that was a luxury, a radio, and there was no
television anyway. Television didn't come out until
1955 or 1956. Things are so open now. I don't know
if that is good or if it is bad. I really don't know.

IV "Strong Tonics:" Coping with Ill-Health

Newfoundlanders, naturally enough, were vulnerable to health crises and chronic illness despite efforts to maintain good health. This chapter illustrates how many managed illness and injury. How did they cope in general? How did they cope with the uncertainties and inconsistent patterns of disease? What resources did they have to call upon?

Coping was helped by the availability of choices. Aside from home remedies galore, there was a range of lay and professional practitioners as well as the neighbourly help we have already considered. The ability to call upon countless beliefs and explanations about diseases was also significant. Today we might call such resources pluralistic. However, these alternatives were being narrowed by the 1950s, partly through changes in medicine and of the health care system as a whole. We do not consider this trend here, nor the increased accessibility it brought to regular medical services and reliance on them. Nor do we consider the contemporary self-care scene as it becomes increasingly pluralistic through the recent growth of interest in alternative care.

Many things influenced how a person coped with an illness. Popular beliefs and explanations served a number of purposes, helping a person to cope or deal with uncertainties. Beliefs help an individual respond to such questions as: "Why me? Why have I caught the disease?" Responses range from common explanations (perhaps acceptable to professional medicine) to the unusual. There were many "causes" from outside the body. Dampness, an everyday concern among informants, could account for a cold, fever, rheumatism, tuberculosis and much more. Germs, emanations, bad drinking water, and fairies—albeit not often mentioned—might account for certain mental illnesses and other complaints. The search for answers also resulted in unusual explanations such as accidentally swallowing a rug tack as a cause of tuberculosis.

Apart from outside agents, weak constitutions were seen as a cause of illness ("being of the delicate type"). There was the gradual build-up of impurities that required blood purifiers as treatment. In fact, problems with the blood accounted for many disorders including the phenomenon of 'the *old hag*,' well known in Newfoundland as a form of paralysis occurring during sleep. ("Stagnation of the blood, doctors claim, causes that.") Such explanations helped to offset views that carried a social stigma, namely that a condition was due to immorality or to poverty arising from one's own moral weaknesses. We believe that the latter explanations were never far from the surface in Newfoundland.

Central to the management of many conditions was an extraordinarily wide range of home medicines. There were always choices to be made, such as deciding on the most comforting medicine for treatment of a chronic cough. This could include any number of cough medicines, tonics, blood purifiers and poultices, or even a cup of hot milk. Although many people today are sceptical about the value of the old remedies—whether, homemade or purchased from the store—their reputation for relieving symptoms must not be overlooked. In fact, in chapter V we see that many elders still have confidence in them, although they rarely use them.

When a problem did not clear up, or it seemed to be an acute condition, or one needing help, advice was generally sought. If family members and neighbours could not help, various healers, local and professional, were called upon. Indeed, we see them as part of the community support system

mentioned in the last chapter. For example, one Newfoundland "doctor" was Gran Reddy, an older woman. She was
sometimes the preferred recourse, even if a nurse or physician were within reach. We have mentioned already that the
authority and accessibility of the latter increased during the
century. Some of it was associated with the growth of hospitals, notably cottage hospitals in Newfoundland.

It seems clear that although medicines and support sys-
tems were important, much depended on the patient's ability
to draw upon "inner strength." Much of this derived from
values such as religious faith, self-sufficiency and acceptance.
While inner strength is highly individual, some of it depends
on how one's family responds to illness. As we consider
coping with an illness, we see—especially in the accounts of
tuberculosis—the hardships and problems that often fell on
the shoulders of families.

Tuberculosis

Tuberculosis had widespread social consequences in Newfoundland from around 1900 to 1960. Perhaps more than
any other condition, it raises questions about a person's inner
strength. Our informants' accounts certainly reveal a variety
of experiences with tuberculosis more vividly than for other
conditions. At the same time, they reveal attitudes towards
the disease and beliefs about its cause. A picture emerges with
various shades of meaning, experiences and apparent con-
tradictions.

We see that surgery was of great benefit where the
mother, who was "too far gone to be put into the San," lived
to be seventy-nine. Her survival was perplexing: "How in the
name of God did that woman live, losing all that blood, and
not getting transfusion?" And there are many memories of
people with "weak" lungs, or who were "delicate." These
reflect a belief in hereditary influences held at the time by
physicians and lay people alike, and rationalized why almost
all the members of some families contracted the disease.
However, some Newfoundlanders were always ready to con-

sider that this was due to a family's own inadequacies and
carelessness, even immorality.

Some informants recollect ideas and practices that ques-
tioned the authority of medicine. Certainly many people
queried the protracted treatment at the San, even suggesting
that "cherry bark" (wild cherry bark), as self-treatment, was
the answer. For many this was not the sole regimen. Not only
were there countless different treatments, but also novenas
and other religious and spiritual supports.

Contradictory experiences and information were always
puzzling. "Extra good food, nourishing food," for instance,
was widely recommended, but was not beneficial in every
case. The fear of catching the disease by close contact—which
may or may not imply an understanding of germs—is very
evident; this is confounded by family members not catching
it. "Father slept with mother the whole time and he lived to
be eighty-six and he also didn't get TB." One informant's
mother thought her tuberculosis might have been the result
of swallowing a tack; confirmation of this seems to have come
from "the doctor" enquiring about the kind of sputum.
Another informant notes that she knows "someone who
worked in the San and never got TB." Environmental causes,
often mentioned by informants, were dampness and chills,
yet sanatorium treatment included cold, fresh air even on
damp days. And there are many observations that people
"weren't too careful." This includes a teacher, suffering from
tuberculosis, who offered private tuition to a student.

Following the many excerpts on tuberculosis, we include
informants' comments on problems such as bleeding, rheumatic fever and children's ailments, arthritis, disabilities,
mental illness and other matters. Many further illustrate ways
of coping with mental and physical problems through resourcefulness and much more.

Yes, it was serious with my sister

Mrs. Julia Collins, b. 1921, Southern Shore
Yes, it was serious with my sister, she used to be
coughing blood. She went to the doctor, there was

one here at the time, and then went to the San for two years, and at that time, it was mainly rest you were getting in the San. I had a friend who painted that picture I have on the wall. She was my first cousin, she went in at eleven and she didn't come out until she was twenty-two. It used to be awful cold there, they used to have the windows open a lot. But the last year my sister was in they did something, they opened her back. I suppose you'd call it an operation, and it was called a "franic." I don't know how to spell it but that was what it was called. [Phrenectomy or phrenic crush, severing or crushing the phrenic nerve to give the lung a degree of collapse and hence partial rest—eds.]

My sister came home after the franic and there was never a bit of trouble with her after. She was never a big, robust person. Well, she was kind of spare, too, because she had a crowd of eight kids.

At one time she wasn't really sickly, not bedridden, she used to be down around the house all the time. And then mother started to cough blood, and she was off to the doctor. There was no X-rays at that time. They said mother was too far gone, they wouldn't put her in the San.

So she was home and she used to have haemorrhages. She didn't have much going for her. She was a small person. I was there then. We had the two grandfathers, and there was always something wrong with older people, they'd always have some kind of a cramp or a pain. But, still, I never minded. But I wanted to be a nurse. I was doing really well in school and I was very disappointed when I had to leave. And mother having those awful haemorrhages and Mary in the San. Father was home in the fishing season, he was home all the time.

Haemorrhage and ice-to-hand

When she'd get these haemorrhages [from the lungs], she'd have to lie down and there was nothing the doctor could do for her. The only suggestion he had, and this went on for years, that they'd put ice on her chest. She had a rubber sheet underneath her. When she would get these attacks, we had a red blanket and we'd put that over her so we wouldn't see the blood when she'd be throwing it.

There was no ice boxes around and in the winter the men would cut the ice off the ponds—that was the only way to get a bit of money in the winter. And there was sawmills here, which are not here anymore, everybody sawed their wood from the forest themselves and built their barns and what have you; and they would buy the sawdust and cover the ice and they'd have that big pile of sawdust in the store, and cover the junks of ice, big junks. It was all according to how frosty the wind was, and saw them up on that pond, there was another pond there too. So that would be stacked there, so then in the spring of the year the vessels would come and they'd buy so much ice to ice their bait to keep it. This time now, we used to have to get someone to come up to Calvert. So Frank was working in the shop, running the shop for Tom Power over there on the beach. It was the only store in Calvert then. The ice house was close to it and the man who owned it gave us ice.

In the winter we didn't need the icehouse because anywhere at all you'd get ice. Put the ice then on her bare chest, that's what the doctor said to do with her. Can you imagine now, four or five pieces of ice on your chest, and that melting and going down? Then mother would change her clothes. For a couple of days she'd be afraid to stir, afraid she'd have another haemorrhage. And then you had all that clothes to wash, and try to move her. She was very small so my father and I would move her and change the clothes.

She went through a lot of that. She had a lot of haemorrhages and she had the sputum.

But she lived to be seventy-nine

I said to the doctor during work in St. John's one time, "How in the name of God did that woman live, losing all that blood and not getting transfusion?" There was no such thing as transfusion then. The doctors weren't wrong or anything because there was nothing they could do for her, that's the way it was. She wasn't going to live anyhow, that's what they thought, but she lived to be seventy-nine. Now each haemorrhage she had, I guess, weakened her. She got in a way that she couldn't sit up and she was afraid, always afraid of her life of haemorrhages. Sometimes then she'd get coughing blood and she'd be right worried. But, you know, that died out, these haemorrhages died out and she never had any more.

She never had the haemorrhage but she continued to cough blood and she would have a large paper bag and toilet paper and you'd fold up the little pads and she had them there on her little table. Whenever she coughed she'd put it down in the bag. She had a pad that she used to write on, she'd ask you stuff that way. That's all she had. She had her bedpan, she had no other problem except headaches sometimes. She'd put Minard's Liniment on her head—she'd just rub it on her forehead. It was a great thing.

She used to wonder, did the tack stick into something?

There was a lot of people died with TB years ago, they said it was TB anyway. But mother used to tell me, she hooked a rug for the stairs and she was putting down tacks and she had them in her mouth while she was putting it down. And she told me she swallowed a tack and she always believed, she used to wonder, did the tack stick into something. I asked Dr. Murphy about it and the first thing he said, "What kind of sputum did she have?" She had that all the time.

We had a big iron boiler and all her clothes went into that and at that time you had lye, it was called, and you would mix that in it and boil the clothes. There was no one in the house got TB. Now, Mary had gotten it before but I looked after her the whole time, brought her meals and changed her bed and washed her, and she was always pleasant, she wasn't hard to get along with, no problem there. I didn't get the disease. Father slept with mother the whole time and he lived to be 86 and he also didn't get TB.

I suppose his lungs must have been weak

There's another thing they used to do years ago. There's a cherry tree grows in the woods. You often heard of a cherry tree. The rind from the cherry tree, it's called cherry bark. People used to boil that, just the rind. You boiled it and that was bottled and that was really good. My cousin, he was supposed to have TB, they were testing him, I suppose his lungs must be weak or something. He's a nice bit older than me now, but he got right thin and miserable looking 'cause there was so much TB on the go. He drank more cherry bark than anyone and he's alive up here in his 80s, up in Renews now. Finest looking man you could see. He claimed it really cured him, 'cause that's all he took. Other people used to take that too.

They weren't careful enough about their food

Sr. Teresina Bruce, b. 1902, Codroy Valley
Most people were healthy but there were a few people who died with tuberculosis. Right next door to me there was a cousin of mine, she was only eighteen or twenty, she died with TB. They looked after her at home. She didn't go to the San, but they put her downstairs in a room where she could be near everybody. They'd tried to give her extra good food,

nourishing food, but she died. There was another cousin of mine farther up the road who also had that. There were two in the family who died from TB and they said when they were sick they weren't careful enough about their food. They would share their food with the sick person.

The doctor didn't know any more than they did

I remember once being sick myself with, I suppose you'd call it the flu or a bad cold or something, and my father getting the horse and carriage and bringing me down to the doctor. I can see that now and could see that then the doctor didn't know any more than they did. He said to keep her warm and give her lots of liquids but anyone would know that anyhow.

He came out in the cold and got chilled; people said about them that they weren't too careful

Mrs. Mary Whelan, b. 1902, Conception Bay
There was one family with TB that they said the eldest boy went to a dance one night, got very much overheated and came out in the cold and got chilled. That's's the way they explained he got TB. He died and his sister about his own age, got TB and lived much longer but she finally died with TB. More of the family seemed to have gotten—I don't know if it was TB—a bad cough or a bad cold, but got over it. They were a great big family and people said about them that they weren't too careful. They weren't too careful about isolating the people with TB and the younger ones were careless about it and would probably spend too much time with them or, as I said, share perhaps a lunch with them.

Get your feet wet and you'd get TB

Mrs. Phyllis Hawkins, b. 1920, Conception Bay
Before I got married, I think TB was a lot on the go then. A lot of people, I know, the sanatorium, that was

filled with people. When we lived in the States, a lot of people had polio then, so you were always in fear of getting that. My mother always said if you stayed in wet clothes, if you went out and got soaking wet, and you didn't bother drying yourself, drying your hair and went to bed, you could develop TB. So you could cause it by doing those things yourself like getting your feet wet. Always make sure you had rubbers on. "Get your feet wet and you'd get TB." These were the things that people were concerned about, that you would get it if you neglected yourself. Diphtheria was there, yes. That's was before I went, when I was young. I heard my mother say that people on the street would have it and they would be quarantined. Yes, typhoid fever, scarlet fever, and all this.

Wash it in lye water. Lye would kill any germs, any TB germs

TB was lung trouble. A lady, in fact, I used to look after her children, she had TB, she didn't go in the sanatorium, she was home, because she had three children. She couldn't look after them, I used to look after them for her. I used a lot of lye water, my mother told me that in looking after this person you don't want to catch any germs, so everything you touch you wash it in lye water, washing dishes, everything like that, put a little drop of lye into everything.

Gillett's Lye, it come in a can, little flakes you had to be very careful over, prevent children from getting at it and keep it up on a high shelf. But take a little bit of that and put it in water and use it in the dishwater and anything, especially with her with TB. And to wash her clothes and everything was always scalded. Now years ago they would use a big pot on the stove, with this lye water, and scald the clothes into it. I don't know if there was Javex then or not, but that's what they used to use. Lye would kill any germs, any TB germs or any other germs. And she stayed home all that time. She didn't go to the sanatorium at all. I don't think she had a doctor.

We used to give her paper bags when she had to cough and spit up things and use the tissues. They were burned then, I had to put them in the stove and burn them. She was in bed all the time. About two years really bad.

Very seldom you'd get a doctor, then you'd go by other people telling you what to do. Now my mother told me what to do, looking after her, saying, "you're looking after that woman, so you have to be very careful you don't catch the disease yourself." So this is what I was doing, I looked after her for two years. Some people were afraid to go near anyone if they had TB, they would hardly speak to them.

She wanted Mom to send me private to her and she sick in bed with TB

Mrs. Phyllis Hawkins, b. 1910, Conception Bay
It was consumption then. Nearly everyone had it, but thank God none of us had it. There was a stigma, being poor, but it didn't have to be that you picked up a germ.

They'd dose with Minard's Liniment or something like that. I had a teacher, the last year, I got honours in intermediate. It was all you could get around here, you'd have to go to St. John's, and then there was no university but you'd go to maybe St. Bon's or Mercy. What was I going to tell you about that? This teacher, the last one I had, had TB and had to give up and go to bed. She was that bad. She knew I was going to pass intermediate and she didn't want the new teacher to get the credit of my passing. Can you imagine it? She wanted Mom to send me private to her, and she sick in bed with TB. Of course, Mom wouldn't send me, regardless of TB.

I know of someone who worked in the San and never got TB. But the windows were open

Mr. Brendan Casey, b. 1922, Bonavista Bay
You can cure TB today. But in our day you went out and laid down in the grass in the bit of sun and that's all. You went out in the San and they opened the windows. I know someone who worked in the San and never got TB. But the windows were open. We'd go in to see friends after we were home here and the windows were open. The fresh air is grand but you got to have some antibiotics or something to cure it up.

It ripened and busted

Mr. Billie-Mike Rossiter, b. 1927, Southern Shore
I remember one, John Glynn. He was a strapping young man born in '22 and he went from a picture of health, athletic physique, to a skeleton and dead within five or six months. And we had a lot of open sores TB. Probably someone hit their knee or stubbed their toe and developed to an infection that would bust and there was no healing in that.

I guess if a person had the TB germ in their body and when they injured themselves and all swolled up, there was an inflammation set in and consequently got to, well, the term they used then was, "It ripened and busted." Most of the time caused death because it never healed and the sore got bigger and bigger and probably struck some vital organ.

To me it was starvation

Mr. Albert Boland, b.1921, Southern Shore
There was a lot of people in Bay Bulls who died with tuberculosis. To me it was starvation, I have no doubt in my mind that killed them all. They used the word tuberculous, which was wrong. I can see them now. I was seven, eight, ten years old, see them little white coffins coming out of the houses with children, for being very sick for six months, a year, and die. Whole

families. Starvation I think it was, and pride, wouldn't go look for help. Contagious? No. The only one I remember was contagious, someone had scarlet fever one time.

I had a first cousin who died of TB. He was an orphan. He went to Mount Cashel Orphanage and he got out of it and was living in old schooners and got wet. Got a chill, and from there developed TB.

They were on kind of the delicate side

Mr. Fergus Babcock, b. 1911, St. Mary's Bay
I'd say they were on kind of the delicate side, many of them with TB, though there's strong people who developed TB. There was a lot on the go then. The sanatoriums were full, sure, with people and then they got that new drug and cleared them all out. Now there is no TB.

I had a brother in there, you know, from Trepassey, a stepbrother. I went in to see him a couple of times and I saw it, not on his bed but a couple of beds down, "Is that snow?" I said.

"Yes, boy, that's snow coming in through the window here," he said. I said, "Why don't you close it?" "No, the doctor said to leave it open to kill the germs, the TB germs. It would survive on the heat but with the cold, you kill it."

Oh yes, cold, yes. Sure, in the sanatorium the snow used to blow in through the window. They have the windows up in the sanatorium all the time. I often went in and saw snow on the beds. "Supposed to have it. That's's the way it's supposed to be," said a girl. And I said, "Don't you mind it?" "No, no," she said, "we don't mind." That's's the way it was in the San.

Mind and body go together, that's part of God's plan anyway, physical and emotional

Sr. Catherine Daly, b. 1899, Placentia Bay
Making a novena or praying the rosary was common

practice for Catholics during times of ill health; using St. Anne's oil, drinking Easter Water, or wearing a particular saint's medal was often part of the treatment. Yes, mind and body go together. That's's part of God's plan anyway, physical and emotional.

A lot of people will say it was God's will, whether it was God's will or not, you accepted it as God's will because it's not God's responsibility all the time when we make mistakes. I'm trying to bring this out with proper language. You had your rosary every evening before the young people would go out, right after supper, supposing you had to leave the dishes until after the rosary. My mother always gave out the rosary until she got sick, then it was brother Tom gave it out. Grace before and after meals. Morning and night prayers.

Indeed they would always pray, make novenas. Great devotion to St. Anne, all Newfoundlanders, I think, had great devotion to St. Anne, the patron of the sick. Have you been at the Shrine of St. Anne de Beaupré? Mrs. Philomena Chafe has pilgrimages to St. Anne's every year for years. She was cured herself, this is her story, and she promised St. Anne that she would bring people to the Shrine; so she organizes, she had two planes, one in June and another in August. What an organizer of a woman, talk about leaders.

I don't know exactly now, I believe it was back trouble but I'm not sure of that. Her cousin is with us, Sister Angela, she is on her holidays now, she would be able to tell us. But that's Philomena's promise to Almighty God, two pilgrimages.

Bleeding

Among the inhabitants of Newfoundland's isolated communities is a relatively high incidence of medical conditions caused by recognized genetic defects. The following excerpt is from a sufferer of one of these, a bleeding disorder, probably a mild case of haemophilia.

I used to bleed a lot

Mrs. Roberta Haynes, b. 1921, Labrador
The only thing I had to see a doctor, I had a tooth out,
for bleeding so bad, but that was the doctor come off
the boat. When I used to get a tooth out when I was
young, before I was married, I used to bleed a lot. I
had a tooth out on board a steamer, but it bled so bad
Mom couldn't stop it and Nurse Parsons was down at
Triangle with her father—he was down there fishing,
and she was down there for a holiday—and she
couldn't stop the bleeding, and they sent like a
telegram then, and the doctor's boat was on the way
from St. Anthony, and the doctor come to see me. But
by the time he got there, it was stopped bleeding. I
got weak because I lost a lot of blood.

This boat was making her trips down on the Labrador, going down and they phoned the fishing ships
harbour and the man there was Lewis Dawe; he was
the merchant and he went out in his boat to talk to the
doctor because he was going on down and wasn't
calling. First they didn't see Lewis Dawe. And he wove
and done everything, and then he said to the man in
the boat with him, "I wonder if I jumped overboard
and they see the man in the water, I wonder would she
stop." Anyway, he managed to stop the doctor's boat.
So he told them about the girl who was bleeding so
bad, had a tooth out, then the doctor came to Triangle.

It used to bleed right free and then it would clot,
but it would clot and fill my mouth out, you know.
Then the nurse would have to take the big clot out
and then it would start bleeding free. A clot would
form so that I could hardly breathe, then take the clot
out, and it would bleed free again. I had a couple of
teeth hauled like that when I was a girl, and I'd bleed
bad and then Nurse Bennett pulled one for me one
time after I came here and we had some job to stop
the blood. I'll tell you, I just remembered, when my

gums were bleeding they went up the Bay and found
a junk of ice, iceberg, and got ice and that's what they
stopped it with. Putting the ice right on my jaw. Off
an iceberg, a small one. Went up the Bay in the boat
and that's how they stopped it.

Children's ailments

High infant mortality has already been mentioned, as has the
role of diphtheria. Rheumatic fever was always a worry if only
because cardiac complications could lead to lifelong invalid-
ism. If scarlet fever caused less of a worry, it still prompted
much concern. ("You could die from that.")

Many old-timers remember quarantine measures. ("We
used to live on a road, and it was all barred off from horses,
nothing could come around.") As much as anything this
encouraged the prudence we have mentioned already. We
see, too, in the selections further emphasis on dampness and
the need to wear dry clothes.

I think that's how I got rheumatic fever

Sr. Catherine Daly, b. 1899, Placentia Bay
Goodness gracious, I just had my mind on it and I
forget it now, rheumatic fever. I was in bed for six
months. The doctor used to come up all the time. We
were on complete bed rest, and had to take our meals
in bed.

We used to get our feet wet and everything. I think
that's how I got rheumatic fever, it was going to school
in the winter; we used to have to walk to school and
walk back. And there were very bad winters then, and
we used to get our feet wet and everything. There
were no gaiters when we were growing up. You only
had the shoes and we had to haul a pair of stockings
over them and put a pair of rubbers on them, that was
all we had. When we got home though, we used to
always change our clothes, put on dry clothes.

It would be better for all hands to get over it the one time

Mrs. Mildred Meaney, b. 1923, Placentia Bay
We all had scarlet fever when we were growing up.
Everybody in the family; as one got it, all hands would
get it. I was about four or five, I suppose. I was some
sick. I remember Mom used to lift me around. It was
a weakness. I couldn't walk for a couple of days, then
you'd get back the strength in your legs again, but
you'd be sick after for a while.

It was just aspirins and orange juice for treatment.
We used to get over it. There was no after effects left.
I said "God used to do all that over on the island when
there was no priest or anything." And we used to
drink a lot of milk, cow's milk. We had our own cow,
we found that good. I'll tell you what we used to do,
boil the milk in the night, a cup of hot milk going to
bed was really good. All the children used to love that,
make you go to sleep. A slice of bread and molasses
too at night. That's was really healthy.

Then we used to get the measles, and mumps and
chicken pox, all that was on the go, probably two or
three would have it the one time; it would be better
for all hands to get over it the one time.

Informants remember minor children's ailments with great
clarity, sometimes because of experiences with their own
children. ("You didn't mind the mumps or any of that was a
mild type.") While tonics or other medicines—home-made
or purchased—are remembered either favourably or with
disgust, many remember that often the biggest problem in
easing the discomfort was how to keep warm. ("We only had
the kitchen stove.")

It was a leaf and you'd steep it.

Mr. Paddy Nolan, b.1919 — Southern Shore
I don't remember taking anything special for it. They
used to have some old medicine like Dr. Chase's and
cod liver oil and stuff like that. They used to have a

build-me-up or a tonic which they called beef iron and wine. Did you ever hear tell of that?

They'd generally have them in for the winter. Well, the old people had funny ideas. Mostly in the spring of the year. They'd clean the blood in the spring of the year. Senna tea and all stuff like that. It was to move your bowels or something like that. That's was the only thing that I know. Senna tea. It was a leaf and you'd steep it. Not very pleasant. I believe you can get that yet.

They used to have prunes and stuff like that. They used to have goose grease. To rub your chest if you had bronchitis or anything like that. Every house used to render the goose grease out and keep it in a bottle to rub your chest.

They'd have molasses and vinegar. That's was a kind of medicine for your chest. If you had a bad chest they'd boil that on the stove. Sugar, molasses and vinegar, I think it was. Everybody had them and all the old people knew about them. Yes, mostly with the youngsters. They'd give them a dose of that in the spring of the year to clean the blood. That's's what their idea was.

Muscle aches, rheumatism, arthritis

Muscle aches, rheumatism and arthritis—the terms were used interchangeably among Newfoundlanders, as else-where—brought much discomfort and frustration among fishermen and, of course, others. Explanations about the cause ranged from dampness to starch. There were many treatment choices including liniments, blood purifiers and tonics.

It's the starch in potatoes

Mr. Fergus Babcock, b. 1911, St. Mary's Bay
It's the starch in potatoes. Arthritis is in the bones and this starch gets in the bones. What you need growing up is plenty of milk, all the milk you can drink. I never

drank tea until I was twenty, all milk, milk, milk. We had a cow and I used to drink all the milk. My grandmother put some in her tea and I would drink the rest. I drank it out of the pan sometimes. I grew up on milk. I never broke a bone; I'm after getting in a lot of accidents, but my bones are solid. You got to drink milk for strong bones.

No arthritis when I was growing up. Nothing. They used to call it rheumatism. A lot of people had it in the back and they had it in the legs. But it wasn't too bad though. They used to walk around. Some days they'd say, "the damp weather would lean on it."

Disabilities

People with disabilities, whether physical or mental, were part of every community. Generally speaking, there seems to have been as much community acceptance of the mentally as the physically handicapped. A person might be a "bit foolish," but this was accepted so long as he or she was harmless to others. Perhaps this was helped by the numerous beliefs and attitudes that existed (and exist) about mental illness. Fairies might steal infants and replace them with mentally deficient or deformed ones. Nervous conditions were also seen as commonplace and helped neighbours to accept those with more severe episodes. Outport people looked after their mentally handicapped at home. However, over time medical treatment at the "Mental" in St. John's became more common.

My older brother Phil, he had a short foot; the delicate type

Mrs. Julia Collins, b. 1921, Southern Shore
Going to the doctor wasn't the thing, though there was a doctor in Ferryland. But he would have to go to Trepassey and Cape Broyle. When my older brother, Phil, came, the doctor was in Cape Broyle and he couldn't leave to come home. When he did finally come home to deliver Phil, it was a bit late anyway,

and there was only one foot came, breech birth, an awful job trying to deliver him.

And he had a short foot. Actually he was crippled. He walked with a limp, something to do with the birth. When the little foot was pulled, I suppose, but his one leg was shorter than the other. So he went right through school and worked on the base, and a big job as an administrator's assistant. He died after with an aneurysm, but he was delicate all the time, the delicate type. He did a lot of clerical work.

There was a lot of crippled people in Ferryland. I remember a long time ago everybody went to the cemetery at Christmas, every Sunday if its fine, especially in the summer when it was always fine. There was one man up in St. John's and he stopped, talking to some gentleman, and he said, "How come there's so many cripples here?"

No one in a wheelchair. No such thing as a wheelchair. They had crutches. There was one old man, he had a little leg, and years ago they used to say the fairies took it. He was about three years old and there was nothing wrong with him, so I guess it was polio. Of course, the mothers would say when the children were out, "You have to come in." They were never allowed out after dark. "Remember Mr. John Joe, now. The fairies took him." That's might have been an excuse to get the children in, too. But he had this little leg and it only came down to his knee, it never grew.

And the little leg used to twist around when he'd be walking with crutches. But he was a wonderful man. He reared the biggest kind of a family. He went to Mass every day of his life. And on Easter, the day Our Lord died, he went to mass from twelve to three. And he went and sat in that church. And in the winter he'd go on his little horse. And he grew all kinds of flowers, every kind of an animal, he even had foxes in a house. He had a rope coming into the house on the back, and when the foxes would start acting up he'd pull the rope and make a sound with the bell he had there and they'd stop. He had geese and hens and if a bird fell and was crippled, everyone would bring down that bird to him. He was a wonderful man. He was a cobbler.

And do you know what he did in the summer? He had a boxcar and a little horse. He worked on the highroads. There was no pavement now, and he'd have to go up in the pits and fill his box with gravel and go along and fill up any holes in the road. And he lived to be an old man. He was my mother's godfather and his son is my godfather, he's alive yet, he's up in his eighties.

I suppose it all could be birth problems

I don't know why there was a lot of people on crutches in Ferryland. I wonder sometimes. There was two more men really crippled like Mr. Hynes and they fished. Imagine going out on crutches and jigging fish. They all got out on a fine day. They would be out talking to the neighbours and visiting, and that's why the guy from St. John's saw so many crippled people, and Phil was one of them. I suppose it all could be birth problems.

We never had time to be depressed

Mrs.Phyllis Hawkins, b. 1910, Conception Bay
You'd hear tell of an occasional one going to the Mental, but not too many. I hear them talking today about being depressed. We never had time to be depressed, we were too busy making a living in our day. What makes people so depressed that they're down and out, what's the reason, there's something on back of it, some trouble? No, everybody was too busy making a living. Nobody could get dole, there was nothing given to you.

The first box of pills wouldn't do much good

Mr. Fergus Babcock, b. 1911, St. Mary's Bay
Nerves, just nerves, that's all. But there were medicines on the go. There was Dodd's Kidney Pills and there was Dr. Chase's Nerve Food. Now, there were black pills and when your nerves would get bad you'd take a couple of boxes of them and you're all right again.

Yes, the first box wouldn't do much good. There wouldn't be many in the box, a little box, a rounded one made out of shaving or something, made out of wood, and you take one and the first one wouldn't do much good but the next one would cure you up.

Yes, called a nervous breakdown. Like I say, I tell you if somebody died who belonged to you, your nerves would get bad after. They used to believe in ghosts and everything then. So they'd think they were still there. The woman or her daughter or son, her nerves would get bad and she couldn't eat or couldn't sleep, so she'd take Dr. Chase's Nerve Food and build herself up and she'd be all right again. Her mind would be on the pills then, her mind would be on getting better and forget about the other. It's all in the mind.

Oh, no, me grandmother and Mrs. Watson and them, they go tell them how they're feeling and they'd tell you to go take the nerve food. And get the nerve food in the mail. Send out to St. John's for it.

Every time she would get pregnant . . . she'd be out and she roaring out

Mrs. Marion Pittman, b. 1925, St. John's
We did have a lady, lived further in the road. Every time that poor creature would get pregnant, in the middle of the night she'd be out and she'd be roaring out, and she'd be calling the husband everything and you'd know when the poor creature was pregnant. It's only about two years ago she died, ninety-six year old.

But when her pregnancy would be over she would be all right. She was a very sad lady because she couldn't help herself and nobody could help her. I suppose they gave her tablets or something, but it didn't ease her down when the spurt would hit her. Very small lady too for the family she had.

Yes, it really is interesting when you look back and see what they got today when they're pregnant. They can tell now, put your stomach in front of the glass and they can see the baby.

There was a girl on the island, not handicapped, childish

Sr. Catherine Daly, b. 1899, Placentia Bay
There was a girl, not handicapped, childish. She was the only one. She lived alone but she went around to houses every day and get a meal here and there, harmless. Mentally retarded certainly. Her mentality was that of a child. She knew how to go around. She looked after herself, but not very well. Mostly they'd come and look after her.

I wasn't home when this happened. I was at the Convent. My brother was telling me, this woman went off, they noticed her doing strange things. In places like that there was a J.P. working for the government, Justice of the Peace. Now my brother, Jim, from my mother's first marriage, he was Justice of the Peace for a while, and if any problems arose they had the responsibility of taking care of it. There was a Constable in Placentia, it was his responsibility to let him know, so he sent a message to him to come over because she was really a subject for the Waterford. She would be dangerous to herself especially.

She was quite a sewer, sew a lot even for the priest, making vestments. They decided she could stay there on the island. But she was living alone, that's why. She wouldn't have anyone living with her, and she had no family. Then she'd start doing outlandish things that she wouldn't do normally. Perhaps she was getting up

in the middle of the night and going up to the church
by herself in the dark. She was really 'mental.' They
were telling me about it.

Then they had a job to get her off. When they were
bringing her around, almost by force, one man on
each side of her, take her up to get her into the boat
to get her over to Placentia, she said, "It's ye should
be going away and not me." She didn't want to go.
Had to bring her in and she would be held in Placentia until you'd get her into the Waterford. They
wouldn't keep her in the courthouse in Placentia
because she had to be treated, so I imagine she went
to the Waterford. But she got better and she remar-
ried in Placentia, Freshwater now, and later on ended
up in St. Patrick's Mercy Home. I met her in there,
quite well.

Never treated as an outcast

Mr. Billie-Mike Rossiter, b. 1927, Southern Shore
It wasn't talked about. That's happened a lot in older
people. They just put it down to senility. Right now it
would be Alzheimers. You'd hear a lot: "That's poor
old man don't know what he's doing—he's senile."
They were included in the community, but if they
tried to take part in the conversation no one paid any
heed. They'd ramble on. Never treated as an outcast.
Violent persons were feared. There was a lot of fear of
someone who was violent.

Some of them got really disturbed and they couldn't be han-
dled at home

In the olden days on this shore we had a policeman
stationed in Bay Bulls, in Cape Broyle, in Ferryland,
in Renews, and each one, like Constable Sulley, Constable Mahoney and Constable Quinlan; these were
the policemen that I knew in my time. The man from
Bay Bulls, he always was a cycle cop and he covered

from Bauline South to Bay Bulls. He had a cycle to travel.

My father was a mailman for awhile here on the shore and at that time there was very little vehicles up here, cars or anything like that. So he brought several people into the Waterford Hospital. Some of them got really disturbed and they couldn't be handled at home so they'd call the police and the police would take them and put a straightjacket on them and get someone with a vehicle to get them to town. Always the police. He was disturbed and he needed to go to the Mental.

I know of two who my father brought in and they're still there. One of them may be dead now. I'm not quite sure. But I know Michael Harrington from Witless Bay. My father brought him out on a horse and slide in the winter, himself and Constable Mahoney.

There was a few that was touched

Mr. Paddy Nolan, b. 1919, Southern Shore
There was a few with mental disabilities but they generally got along alright. They just had a theory that the worst time they'd be would be on a full moon. It used to happen. But I never knew anybody really bad that they had to put away or anything. There was a few that was touched a little bit. They might make a few jokes about them or something.

They just kept it to themselves. One looked after the other during the bad times. There was no doctor to go to and most people couldn't afford to see a doctor. It wasn't very much at the time but they'd have to be really bad when they'd take them to St. John's. Then they'd have to go over the road on horse and cart or slide in the winter. They generally got someone with the best horse, the fastest horse, and a couple would go with him. It would take them about five hours to get to St. John's.

Practitioners: variety galore

Earlier we indicated that Newfoundlanders can be said to be pluralistic in their health care. This is well illustrated by the variety of practitioners, including non-professional, they called upon for advice or treatment. Of course, as many narrative excerpts have already made clear, choices were limited in practice, since getting professional help in a hurry was often impossible for outport Newfoundlanders:

Mrs. Geraldine Reddy, b. 1903, Placentia Bay
You couldn't get access to a doctor, you had to wait weeks, months, to see a doctor, because there weren't that many, they were scarce. And you didn't have the money, another thing, even a dollar or two.

Much reliance was placed on experienced people in a community, some who were always ready to apply a splint, or who possessed "special powers." There were charmers, midwives and others. One senses they were often preferred over regular physicians. However, there was often uncertainty over whether or not a physician should be called. This was especially so as the authority of medicine grew during the first half of the twentieth century. Although our informants offered few recollections about making decisions on who should be called in first, favourable attitudes were often given to local healers. Many people had mixed experiences with regular doctors; although some of them were revered more than clergy, others were viewed as not particularly competent, or were disliked for behaving like they were "God's gift to the universe." Yet all doctors had tests and medicines, often new, which Newfoundlanders viewed as desirable because they were "modern."

Negative comments about physicians were often coloured by confidence in one's own self-sufficiency ("I think they didn't need doctor's medicine a lot in those days"). Yet numerous frustrations have been reported, particularly over bad experiences ("Mom wouldn't use the medicine because she thought that's what killed Bernard") and questionable physician behaviour. These could reinforce negative comments, even if it was said in jest, as in the popular Newfoundland song, "Hard Times." In this, the doctor sàys "he will cure you of all your disease, but when your money he's got, you can die if you please."

Doctor's "time" was and still is an issue. Many people want a doctor to be unhurried, to demonstrate that he or she is not rushing, and to give a "straight answer." Our 1993 informants echo findings in an earlier study among inhabitants of Botwood, Newfoundland. This revealed reasons why the late Dr. Twomey was widely revered:

> *Mrs. Viola Gushue, b. 1930, St. John's*
> Oh, I don't know what to say about Dr. Twomey. He was always there for you. No matter how busy Dr. Twomey was, if you came in and you had a problem other than medical, he had time to sit in his office and talk to you, even if it meant working extra hours . . . Oh, he was grand. I used to love to go to see him. I usually made the last appointment in the afternoon because I was working and he'd sit and chat about everything under the sun. Everything but what was wrong with me.

> One difficulty, often frustration, for rural Newfoundlanders was the turnover of doctors, many of whom were from overseas en route to other places. ("You couldn't get a skilled doctor in a small place like that.") Changes in medical care raised questions about whether or not existing practices represented second class medicine. ("They have confidence in the doctor, but they go to Port-aux-Basques for X-rays.") Uncertainty was constantly interwoven with hope and faith in a doctor's ability to help.

The following excerpts reveal a spectrum of attitudes toward practitioners, lay and professional. Although people often chose one or the other type of practitioner, according to the medical problem and circumstances, comments on lay practitioners and midwives are placed first. We believe that the positive recollections reflect that the individuals were part of the community, that they belonged to the community. In fact, they were in sharp contrast to many physicians in rural Newfoundland, who like one Englishman, remained a "foreigner." Indeed, physicians who became well regarded were often those who came from, or melded into, a community. ("You didn't think he was a doctor at all, the way he was talking, but you'd do what he told you anyhow.")

One quotation below is of special interest today because sexual abuse is such an issue. One informant indicates that she would slap a doctor if he transgressed sexual boundaries with her. To deal with the issue on the spot, so to speak. This seems to reflect the pragmatic mind set of many older Newfoundland women.

We sent for Uncle Michael Rourke

Mrs.Phyllis Hawkins, b 1910, Conception Bay
Now my brother cut off his finger at the chopping block. There was a little bit of flesh left. There was no doctor to go to, we sent for Uncle Michael Rourke, he came and put Frank's finger on. He never lost his finger, I don't know if he stitched it or what he did, but he never lost his finger and it was hanging. He's eighty-two now.

Yes, he'd come, Uncle Michael Rourke that is, whatever the case might be. He'd put broken bones together. Charged for nothing, nobody had the money to give him. Today, everything, you got too much.

There was a lot of what you could call charmers

Mr. Billie-Mike Rossiter, b. 1927, Southern Shore
There was a lot of what you could call charmers. I have a sister-in-law, Hannah, people come from all over the shore. Doctors sent people to her. She won't tell me what she does. A lady, Teresa Ryan, passed it on to her. She'd cure warts. There was one boy in particular, came from Ferryland. If you want to see

hands—they were ugly to look at. And he had gone to doctors and doctors and doctors. They burnt them off and everything. His mother brought him down to Hannah and in two weeks they were gone.

There was another woman. I was probably eight or nine years old. So I went up to her and she told me to go and get a piece of sheep's wool or sheep's yarn, not washed, with the grease still in it. I went up and when she had finished she gave me it and she said, "Now you bury that and make sure anyone don't see you burying it." She didn't put the wool on the warts. For every wart she tied a knot on the sheep's wool. That's one of the processes but you're not to tell. And you can't release where you buried that wool or what she did otherwise. They went in a week or a week and a half. I never had a wart since.

Now, Hannah, she used to come here to Bay Bulls probably two weeks of the summer for her holidays and she'd come three or four times during the year, maybe for a weekend. She was my mother's lifelong girlfriend. Every time she came to Bay Bulls there was always three or four people because they'd come and ask Mom, "When is Hannah coming up again?" And she'd see them, she'd be here Sunday and three or four people come with warts.

People have gone to Hannah and they more or less laughed at it and Hannah told them, "I can't cure you." Maybe three or four times they'd come back with a different attitude towards it. Amazing, you know. Doctors have sent them to Hannah. Dr. Martin, when he practised in Ferryland, Dr. von Waldenburg, when he was practising here, Dr. Gloria Tong. . . And Hannah has had Anglican people come and they had the belief and they went.

We also had a man here, Mr. Earle Williams. He's dead now, but he stopped bleeding. Once I fell and struck a sharp rock there on my forehead. He stopped the bleeding. Just like that. He stopped the bleeding in three instances in myself. He had a spe-

cial prayer. He'd usually hold his fingers over us. And
five minutes after, no blood. Anyone who had a bad
cut or anything went to Mr. Earle. He had a special
power or something, but it worked. Yes, or maybe
there was something in his touch. There may have
been something in his genes that caused the blood to
coagulate.

Oh, my Grandmother. She was an old nurse, yes

Mr. Fergus Babcock, b. 1911, St. Mary's Bay
Oh, my Grandmother. She was an old nurse, yes. My
dear, she had a bag. No one could see into that bag.
Whatever she had in the bag she used to take it with
her and we never knew. If I had been a girl instead of
a boy she would have told me a lot more than she told
me. She'd say, "If you were a girl now I'd tell you
different things," but she wouldn't tell me, because I
was a boy and that isn't in my line unless I intend to
be a doctor or something like that.

She was given something else besides money if they
hadn't got it. But then there was some couldn't pay
her at all and she used to say "That's all right, don't
worry about it." She was that type, you know. She
didn't care about money. She didn't care about nothing so long as she was healthy and happy and making
everyone else happy. That's was the kind of woman
she was. Oh, she was a real loving woman. Everyone
loved her. Young girls who's getting married came to
see her and they put their whole trust in her, like she
was a god. A great big woman she was. You look at her,
you'd be afraid of her. But she was mild; and she
couldn't read or write, but you still couldn't fool her.
No way you could fool her.

Well, they'd do stuff for her. They'd come to see
her and give her a hand and do something or something like that. Return the favour if they hadn't the
money. Oh, they always had some money, yes, because they used to fish up there and there was a lot of

fish up there. And then in the fall of the year they used to sell a lot of sheep. Butchers came in over the roads for truckloads of sheep and lambs and that and they used to sell them and if they owed Granny any money they would come and pay her. Sometimes she'd give back some of the money to them. "That's's all right now. Here, take some of that back now, that's good enough, that'll be all right."

The whole thing with the baby was $5.00, that's all. Five dollars was a lot. She'd born the baby, then go back and forth to the house for nine days or something. She'd be out doing gardens and stuff like that; and neighbours would come and give her a hand or she'd hook a mat; they'd come, and give a whole day hooking or something like that. She was in with everybody.

They'd get her for about ten days beforehand

Sr. Teresina Bruce, b. 1902, Codroy Valley
My own grandmother was a midwife. I remember somebody saying when there was a baby coming they'd get her for about ten days beforehand and she'd live with the woman and then she'd direct her to what she was to do and how she was to get along. She'd stay with her for the actual birth and perhaps a week afterwards. Her sister, who was my great-aunt, was another midwife.

There was a Mrs. Tomkin. I boarded with her when I was teaching. She had great confidence in my grandmother. She'd come there and stay with her and if she got a pain, she'd probably give her hot water or get something hot and put it on her stomach. Very, very simple remedies, but they worked.

I don't think there was any special fee. Later on when I was grown up there was a lady who lived close to us who went somewhere and took a course in midwifery. I don't say that was the very latest thing but she did have a course and she did a lot of that sort of work afterwards and you paid her or I think she had a government grant.

Grandmother and great-aunt just learned from experience. I think some of these old ladies had a special knack. Perhaps you have a knack for music and I have a knack for needlework. They seemed to have a God-given gift for nursing. They seemed to know by instinct just what to do.

Uncle Jim Devereaux

Mr. Jerome Murphy, b. 1911, Conception Bay

Uncle Jim Devereaux, he could set a bone, but I don't remember anyone in our area breaking bones. The bones must have been good and hard because there was none broke in our family. There was a woman, too. They used to go to her but not that many. Old people from over here used to go to her; she could mix a salve to put on a boil or something like that.

She borned an awful lot of babies

Mrs. Roberta Haynes, b. 1921, Labrador

Mother, she worked as a servant, a maid, for a short while before she was married. Probably the woman was expecting and had a small baby and needed someone for a while to come in and do some work. Mom was a good help for Daddy getting the logs. I can remember when I was a child growing up, Mom would be down at the stage when they'd get a lot of fish and probably wouldn't get it put away, the fish done, until one o'clock in the night. And I'd be up home rocking the cradle. Mom told me she often came in and seen me sound asleep on the floor and my hand still on the cradle when I'd be rocking the baby. I'd sooner be out of doors trying to make money that way, working. I went probably for two or three days and work like that. But I'd sooner be jigging the fish and catching the fish and drying it and get stuff for myself.

If anyone got sick, you'd go and do what you could, go and help out, help one another and do the best they could. My mother, she was a midwife. She borned Ivy, my oldest daughter. Yes, she was a midwife for years, after she got her own family just about grown up.

And her mother was a midwife for years before her. She borned an awful lot of babies, Grandmother Penney. Mom's father was from Newfoundland, she was born down in Labrador, because he married a girl from Labrador and lived down there. Mother became a midwife after her own family was born. The doctors and nurses wasn't there, so midwives had to do the work. And they used to have to go around, if those small communities didn't have a midwife, in the fall before the Bay would freeze up. They was afraid it wouldn't be froze up enough to get a midwife, then they'd take the midwife and perhaps she'd have to stay a couple of months, waiting, if there was no midwife in the settlement.

The priest would bless their hands and everything

Mrs. Mildred Meaney, b. 1923, Placentia Bay
I had children at home. I had two in the hospital because we moved over here. With those at home, it was nothing, only midwives, no doctors. The midwives delivered the baby, that's all there was to it. She'd stay with you three or four days after. She was a wonderful woman. When she gave up, a couple of more women took it up; they went and took the classes in St. John's. And the priest would bless their hands and everything. They'd never charge anything. You'd give something, if you had something you'd give it to them, probably a meal of your home made potatoes or something like that and they'd be so delighted to get that, or probably a dried fish or something, something in return.

To deliver the baby, they'd have boiling water and

lots of towels, that kind of stuff. Them times they used to keep us in bed for eight or nine days, now in the hospital you're up after the next day. That's was the style then, they wouldn't let you up, afraid you'd get a cold or anything. No, we never had a complication, thank God. When Peter was born, I had to get a doctor then. What happened to me, something happened? After Peter was born, I think it was the after-birth or something, it wouldn't come and they had to get a doctor. They went and got the doctor in St. Mary's and he came up. It took only a few minutes once he came. This was over on the island. Only about an hour or so to come. He came from up in St. Joseph's then. We didn't have it too bad. Nobody died for the want of a priest or a doctor over there.

They just left their house and came down

Mr. Charles Tarrant, b. 1921, Southern Shore
I do remember a good bit about it because there was an old lady over here, a midwife, a Mrs. Bouden. She was as good a woman I think as you could find and she had a stepson Bob and they had a horse. So Mrs. Jones, or whoever the case may be, Mr. Jones walked up from North side in the night, probably in the stormy winter, "Will Mary Ann come down, the wife is having a baby? Have you got a horse?" "Oh, no, we have no horse." So Bob was called then and he went up in the barn and tackled her own horse and came down to the house and "wait now, child, there's an old blanket upstairs." And that poor creature had nothing to make diapers out of. "I'll bring down the blanket now and I'll make some diapers while I'm at nothing else." That's the type of woman she was.

We had a baby born 8 years before, early anyway and she stayed over here. Ann had to go to the hospital out in St. Clare's. We had to get a lend of the priest's car and she came out with us and stayed in St. Clare's that night and when he was bringing home the priest's car in the morning, the driver, she came with him. Went over, how much you going to charge me? "Oh, nothing, child. I don't charge anything." And I gave her a pair of slippers, so that's what she got for all that work.

They had another midwife down North side, a big fat woman, I suppose she was nearly 300 pounds. Ann would know more about her now, a Mrs. Canning, and every time she came to the house as a midwife, she had a big white apron with a big pocket in it and there was always something in the pocket. We used to be delighted to see her come, put her hand down in the pocket and there was a candy or something. Mrs. Canning now, that would be about 70 years ago.

In the midwife now, there was another lady down alongside of Murphy. She was a great woman to work and when she went, the mother in bed with the child and no way to look out for anything and not only did she do the midwife job but she cooked and sewed for the children and worked there besides and generally got nothing for it. Some of these midwives had families of their own and they just left their house and came down and, if it was necessary, stayed at the house for 3 or 4 days until the woman got a bit better.

The green scapular is a religious thing

Mrs. Betty Corcoran, b. 1925, Southern Shore
Of course, too, I'm a great believer in prayer. On those lines, there's no point in a person believing in prayer—I'm not a Christian scientist by any means—if you just stay back and say, "Dear God, make me well," and then sit back in a chair and expect your prayer to be answered, that tomorrow you're going to get up and go out and go skiing. You'll have to do your part in conjunction with prayer. There's no sense in me saying, "I got a bad foot, I can't walk. Dear God, make me walk," and *you* do nothing about it. I think that plays a big part in my life too.

I remember, we had a neighbour and she was bleeding after childbirth. The doctor was in Ferryland at the time and we got on the road in the ambulance and it was only four or five miles. And between Portugal Cove and Capahayden the woman said to me, "Mrs. Corcoran, I'm bleeding to death." The perspiration was just coming out and the blood running on the floor, but I had a green scapular and the medal of St. Anne in my bag. I never asked the lady her religion or anything, but when I saw the blood coming, when she held on to me and said she was bleeding to death, I said, "Now my love, I don't know what religion you are, but here's the green scapular, and you put your faith in that, you'll be alright, don't you worry, the green scapular stops the blood." I said, "You believe in that and you'll be alright."

It's a religious thing. I laid the scapular here and I said to the ambulance driver not to stop for nothing, only get to the doctor. We got to him and he was expecting us and he was right there and got in the ambulance. He went right in for the placenta and he couldn't get it. But before he did, just as he looked at the mother, he said, "My dear your bleeding is stopped, what did she give you to stop your bleeding? And he saw what blood she lost, it was on the floor of the ambulance. But he said, "You still got to go into St. John's." So we got on the road and took her into St. John's, St. Clare's, and she went right into the operating room of course. I never used to think about what the doctors did or anything, the only thing bothered me was to get them to the hospital, then I was so happy. But the doctor sent out word to tell me he wanted to see me. When he came out, he asked me where I got my training. I said, "Doctor, I didn't get any training, only what I learned myself from medical books from Nurse Abernathy." I was so curious. I always wanted to find out what to do. That's woman lived and her baby lived and it be premature.

The green scapular stopped the blood. There's one in my purse somewhere, it's just a little green scapular with a picture of Jesus on it.

You ought to know, doctor, you said I'd grow out of it, but I grew into it

Mrs. Mary Whelan, b. 1902, Conception Bay
About my arm, it was pulled out when I was a baby in the cot. My brother pulled me up by the arms and that bone came out. I got a crooked arm. The doctor came around that time and said, "She'll grow out of that" so when I got to be a young woman, good and saucy, he come into the house one day and I was knitting. He said, "What's the matter with your arm?" I said, "You ought to know, doctor, you said I'd grow out of it, but I grew into it. Look at it now." Of course, when I got hardy enough, sense enough to know it was an injury, it was too late. They'd have to break the arm altogether and put it back in the right place. When I'm knitting any length of time, that gets right hot, like an infection in the bone. I can't use a steel needle at all, I got to use a plastic needle. Times I have to get a pill for the pain because I can't sit down and do nothing.

I'm not a doctor lover

Mr. Billie-Mike Rossiter, b. 1927, Southern Shore
I'm not a doctor lover. I'd be really sick before I'd go to a doctor. You got better things to do with your time than wait in a doctor's office. My belief about that is, if you're not feeling well and you start worrying about it, and the doctor gives you something for it, you're only compounding it. That's my philosophy. Half the things you'd go to a doctor for, if you'd stay home for a day or two, it would be gone away. Especially now, since Medicare came in, I'd say fifty percent of the doctors' time is taken up with hypochondriacs.

The doctor was next door to God

Ms. Sally-Ann Myrick, b. 1917, St. John's

The doctor was next door to God. The doctor was better than the clergy or anything else. If the doctor told you to jump, the only thing you'd say was, "How high, Sir?" The doctor was law.

Your doctor was your family, no matter what. It was like going to confession. You went to the doctor, same thing. That's how you were reared up too. There was no sense in you going to a dentist or a doctor if you weren't going to talk to him.

If the doctor was called in, you followed his orders and that was mostly in bed and medicine three and four times a day. Follow orders—strip down. How was he going to examine her if he didn't touch her? Some are like my doctor and some don't bother.

It's like the case where the lady went into the doctor and he put his hands on her breasts. I thought that was a riot. How was he going to examine her if he don't touch her? A doctor should never be tried for something like that. If you go to a doctor and he tells you to strip, you're going to do it, aren't you? If you go in for a thorough examination, which I did, and I had to take everything off but the panties, I don't think he did anything objectionable, otherwise he would have been slapped right hard. And if you don't trust your doctor, who are you going to trust? You can't even trust your church today, you know that.

They think they're God's gift to the universe

They think they're God's gift to the universe. The only doctor I go to now is Dr. Vaughan. I won't be going there again till November, because I have to have my driving license renewed. I think he's fantastic myself. He'll sit and talk to you and answer questions which some of them won't do. But he just seems to enjoy patients coming and talking to him about anything, any matter at all. I find him marvellous. He never hurries you. You go in to him; well, he'll give you a certain time, but you might be an hour waiting to get in. I know that when I go there because he has two nurses on all the time. They'll tell you, "Now, Mrs. Myrick, you're coming in at such a time"; I said, "Don't worry about it, I know I might have to wait an hour or so." I have to wait my turn. And you might go in and be in there two or three minutes, somebody else might be in there half an hour or more. Some people are curious, they like to sit and talk.

Some of them are like my doctor and some of them just don't bother. I have a friend in the Health Sciences Centre, they were on holidays and they had to come back, she went to her knees with pain; and in Gander they couldn't find anything wrong with her, so they were going to send her to Stephenville, but her husband figured out it was just as easy to go home as it is to go to Stephenville. She's in the Health Science now, she got a stone in her kidney. That's brought her to her knees in pain. They'll know today, they're hoping she'll pass the stone; it depends on how many are there. But even doctors don't know everything, they can't say if it's one or more.

The only time they had a doctor was if there was a birth

Mr. Paddy Nolan, b. 1919, Southern Shore
There was no doctor. You couldn't call a doctor. They mostly had their own remedies. The only time they had a doctor was if there was a birth in the family or something like that. They had a doctor in Bay Bulls, Dr. Whelan. He had one leg. Him and a midwife would come and the child would be born and you wouldn't see a doctor until the next one. He had half of the Southern Shore to look after. He'd come in the horse and buggy.

Today it's too easy to go see a doctor. They don't have to make home medicine these days. You don't have to do it today. It was handed down from generation to generation and it worked. That's's all they had; they had faith in it and it worked.

First thing he'd ask, did they have the money to pay?

Mrs. Joyce Burry, b. 1907, Conception Bay
Everybody didn't have a telephone, but thank God we had it; it was out in the back porch as you came in, that's where it was put. If someone wanted the doctor they'd come first to telephone for the doctor. First thing he'd ask, did they have the money to pay?

"There is something wrong because your eyes gave it away"

Jimmy was born in the Grace Hospital, and Marg was five years in the difference, they were both born in the Grace and I had Dr. Roberts, a good old fellow. I was pretty bad when Jimmy was born; after he was born, they had said to me you can go home tomorrow. That's was in the morning; three-thirty in the afternoon, the nurse couldn't believe the thermometer, I said, "Is there anything wrong?"

She said, "No." I said, "There is something wrong because your eyes gave it away." I had an infection where the baby was born.

What happened was a nurse, whether she was a grad or not I don't know, left a swab. I've been through everything, but nothing ever bothered me, I came out of it. I had to stay in hospital another week or more. They got the infection cleared up. Dr. Roberts, he had nothing to do with it, and I was so mad that he had another doctor help him, and they had the priest there and they had them all there, but I wouldn't die, I wouldn't satisfy them.

The next time I went to Dr. Roberts, he had retired. And he said see whoever his assistant was. I said, "If I wanted your assistant I would have gone to him in the first place." I said, "You brought me through when I was bad and if you meet the same obstacles I have enough faith to think that you could overcome it again." "Well," he said, "if you got that much faith in me, I can't let you down." He said, "I'll be there."

The nurses were there in the delivery room and they had to wait awhile and they were frightened to death because he was a fussy old fellow. And he sat there and he never said a word and when I got better, I was bad, they had to walk me and do everything with me, they said, "What kind of pull did you have with Dr. Roberts? I said, "None." Only I had faith in him and I told them. That's man was wonderful.

He's an Englishman, I think, a foreigner anyhow

Sr. Teresina Bruce, b. 1902, Codroy Valley
We had doctors. For most of my growing up there was a resident doctor, but if I may say this, they didn't amount to much. You couldn't get a skilled doctor in a small place like that. You couldn't support them I suppose. So we had doctors that weren't quite finished. Maybe I'm just guessing at that, or doctors that had not made good somewhere else. As far as I remember them, they didn't amount to much.

I remember three doctors we had. One of them used to drink. The other didn't seem to know too much and nobody seemed to have any confidence in him so gradually they left and we got along without them. They do have a regular doctor now in the Valley. They think he's good. I don't know myself. They have confidence in the man, but they go to Port aux Basques for X-rays and more particular examinations. They have confidence in him. He's an Englishman, I think. A foreigner, anyhow.

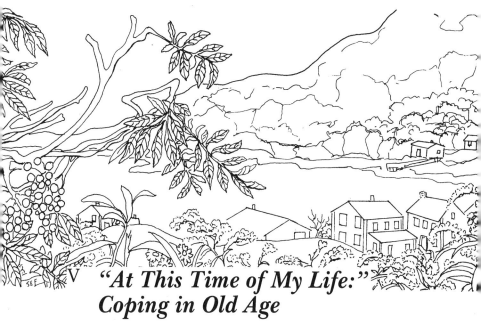

"At This Time of My Life:"
Coping in Old Age

O ur elders recognize that the society and the natural environment of Newfoundland have been greatly transformed during their lifetimes. The way of life most of them knew in small rural and coastal communities has been dramatically reshaped. They attended single-room schools, lived under the influence of powerful churches, helped parents with the fishery and subsistence living. No longer is there the same frugality and self-sufficiency such as we met in the recollections on nutrition; no longer is the same emphasis placed on hard work and clean living; no longer is strong Irish Catholic and conservative Protestant morality so evident, especially in women's issues. As well, various beliefs and practices have been transformed; age-old maxims on exercise and hygiene are now "repackaged" as part of new lifestyle programs. Although elders keep some of their traditional beliefs such as "Keep your feet warm," some informants say that both the problems and blessings of isolated communities are something of the past. Yet, as Newfoundland has become, through television and other ways, part of the "new" global village, there are new concerns and stresses in everyday lives.

These changes lead us to ask whether the values associated with the elders' upbringing and working lives in Newfoundland remain with them to help them cope in their current situations. Such values were self-sufficiency, resourcefulness, pragmatism, prudence, religious faith and acceptance. Interpreting such matters is difficult because of the differing circumstances and experiences of each individual. Some are discomforted by change; others are comfortable with modern developments and seem to have consciously discarded much of their past, or at least do not want to remember it. As they make clear, all informants appreciate recent medical developments. Some, however, are concerned with the rapid rate of change and believe that it is extinguishing important values.

As we listened to our informants' commentaries —particularly their thoughts on differences between generations —we felt that, despite their diverse situations, they have generally retained their Newfoundland values. They may not be able to implement them, but they contribute to a sense of place and identity in the changed circumstances of old age. The values also help the informants to cope as they face vulnerability, social marginalization, and new health concerns. Longstanding values offer positive recollections of past accomplishments in trying times. This gives a sense of who one is—a sense of identity —which, in turn, helps with accepting, accommodating or adapting to new situations. Although the memory of past lifestyles and associated values sometimes heightens a sense of loss, we believe that the values contribute to psychological well-being.

Selecting short narrative pieces from the large amount of data to illustrate our conclusions is not easy. Our interpretations emerge from listening to, as well as reading, the fifteen hundred or so pages of narratives as a whole. Nevertheless, we offer an array of comments that indicate persistence of values amid change. We open with a lengthy narrative that comments on changes in Newfoundland life and underscores certain longstanding characteristics. Self-sufficiency, for instance, is grounded upon a belief in a natural, self-sustaining system of relationships where Mother Nature rules. Following the narrative, short excerpts are grouped to emphasize various themes. For example, under the heading, "Today is different," feelings are expressed about the present, such as the elderly living in their own homes and fear of incapacitating illness (including those "new" to society such as AIDS and Alzheimer's). These selections reflect pride in the past and disquiet with today. Next, under "Memories, roots and recipes for healthy living," we include quotations from informants who remember the past favourably. Although their medicines are rarely used nowadays, they are a readily recoverable part of many elders' memories. They suggest attachment to the past and continuity of values, as do the recommended practices for a healthy life.

The final selections, on "Liberal lifestyles, consumerism and worries over the next generation," specifically contrast the past with the present in terms of liberal thinking, materialism and commercially based comforts. In some ways, these quotations can be seen as a peroration from our elders; they make explicit what is implicit in so many of their stories, a comparison of past values with those of the present. The judgements can be read as a reminder of warnings from elders about rapid social change and a need to examine critically the "new" values that have appeared.

What I'm concerned about is our country

Mr. Fergus Babcock, b. 1911, St. Mary's Bay
I'm keeping the way I am. I am not worrying, I was brought up not to worry, keep moving the way I am. When you get sick, you get sick and if you don't, you don't, so don't worry about it, keep on the go. Keep walking, keep eating and keep sleeping. Keep singing and keep doing things. Forget about it. It's all in the mind.

What I'm concerned about is our country, our island and the way things are going. I don't like it. For a start, they're giving away the food from the codfish. They're starving the codfish. The next thing, we're going to have none because codfish are going to eat one another, because they're giving away the caplin. That's what the codfish builds theirselves up on now after spawning. The salmon now is coming and the salmon builds up on the caplin, then they run to the river and spawn, but now they have nothing there. They're giving the spawny caplin and that's the food of the codfish. Codfish will eat one another. My grandfather caught the biggest codfish ever caught in Newfoundland and in his stomach was another codfish. But that's just before the caplin come. Because you catch them on herring bait then. The codfish were after the herring then, see. But that's their food. Now they're giving it to the Japanese and the fish is eating one another. What the seals is not eating, the codfish is eating, one another they're eating the small ones.

No, millions of caplin coming in and blocking the place and there was loads of fish. The fish comes in behind them. Mother Nature runs it this way and you study it up and you'll find out that Mother Nature is the ruler. Where do the ocean go when it falls? Look how fast it comes back. No one figured that out. You take Riverhead, St. Mary's. There's nothing comes in that arm, that big open arm wide to the sea, only just herring and if codfish come in or any other fish, they wouldn't be able to do what they have to do like their mating and spawning and that once a year, they wouldn't be able to do it, so there's no codfish comes in, nothing only just herring. Holyrood Arm up here, nothing comes in there only squid at a certain time of the year. That's big opening ocean, fish can come in there, but they won't because squid comes in and they does the same thing. So that's Mother Nature. Now the caplin comes to the beaches and spawns and after they go back, the codfish start catching them up. Well, they're after spawning. Next year then, all them will come to life and we'll have more caplin again. But now it's finished. They catches them way outside now, they'd never get to the beaches. By and by, we will have nothing. That's what I am worried about, what I am concerned about.

We could cope with the Depression

I worries about that stuff, yes. Now around the bay, we used to grow our own vegetables, our own cattle and there's nothing up there now. No vegetables up there now, there's no cattle up there. So I can't see what people's going to do when the Depression comes. They won't be able to live. They'll be dying like rats because they'll be so weak, they won't be able to cope with it. We could cope with the Depression that time because we had lots of vegetables, we had lots of cattle.

They made it with what they had. I cut the tail of a horse of a mare we have, I cut the tail of her to make a brush for me grandmother, just as good as you'd buy in the store today. I could make it better than I can now. And I had no tools. All I had was a piece of wire. And I'd sit down, well, I had to cut out the shape of the brush and then I'd sit down and hotten me wire into the stove, into the grates of the stove, the old Waterloo stove, and I'd put it through and then I'd hotten it again and put it through again till I bored all me holes and then I'd get me line and lace it, like, make loops and fit it with hair and put it back. Cut it off and then I had me brush.

We believe in medicine today, yes, but not as much as we did way back. Because like the fella said, it was ground into you and that was it. But now, half the people going now says the doctors and the drugstores is doing just to make money and they don't care how you feel, but them days there was no money involved at all. It was just the medicine. They really go after the complaint you had and give it the whole thing and you believed in them and it got better.

Oh, no, you don't mind. Now, you have no other choice. That's the way it goes now, but see, they haven't got the same faith as they had then. You wouldn't be scared or nothing them times because they'd talk to you and tell you and you were all right.

Me grandmother used to talk Irish like. She'd say, "Ah, you'll be all right, boy, sure, nothing wrong with you at all." I had a pain in me stomach today and I said, "Oh my, I got some pain in me stomach today, I can't go to school." "Ah, that'll be all right now, lie down." She'd get a plate and put it on the stove and hotten it and then she'd get a piece of rag and she'd cut it off and she rolled it up and put it on me stomach. Oh, boy, it would be some hot. Not too hot, no, that's not too bad. "All right now, a few minutes and you'll be all right." It passed away. Probably be only gas, or something I was after eating or something like that. But after a while. So that's faith for you right away.

Down in the court house. I was called in on the grand jury. They picked me for foreman. Like the fella says, I does a lot of talking and yakking and that, so they figured I'd be the best. So I was on that for a year. Now I'm too old to go on anything.

You see, most of this stuff is all in the mind. Your mind does a lot for you and, like I said, if you keep exercising and keep your mind occupied, instead of thinking about yourself and thinking about this and that, and I'm going to get this and I'm going to get that, you know, that sort of slows down the body. But if you're out going, you don't have time to think about this stuff.

Keep your mind occupied

Exercise is the best care of anything. Walking and exercising you haven't got time to be sick. You'll only be sick lying around thinking about yourself. But if you get out and get going, get exercising, it's all in the mind, see.

Another thing. Keep your feet warm. Look after your feet. Because, look at it this way, you can put on a pair of woollen socks and a pair of rubbers, and nice and warm feet, you won't get a cold.

I've been smoking since I was ten years old. Me grandfather used to smoke, me uncles all smoked, and they told me it's good for you. And Dr. McGrath said there's nothing wrong with it, couldn't hurt you. My lungs are perfect! Yes, I can take an X-ray now and show you me lungs. They are just as good as they were when I was twenty years old.

Today is different

In the old days all old people stayed at home

Mr. Jerome Murphy, b. 1911, Conception Bay
In the old days, all the old people stayed at home, the youngest son probably owns the place and the parents stayed there with him. I think they have a better way of life just the same. They enjoyed life better, they contributed and did what they could do, with cutting a bit of wood or feeding the cattle or doing something like that, that the old people could do. It was a way of life.

I said, "No, thank you"

Mrs. Betty Corcoran, b. 1925, Southern Shore
Today is different. Some doctors are really wonderful doctors, and there's others. It was only a few years ago I went over to St. Clare's because I was after having attacks of angina, the doctor told me with any pains at all to go over to the hospital because it could be leading to a heart attack. This evening I had pains and I went over and this doctor, he was on. He examined me and he turns around and he said, "This is what's wrong with the country today," he said, "wasting the taxpayers' money, people coming in here and nothing wrong with them."

It struck me so hard because I had six sons and a husband, working all their lives, half their cheques used to go in taxes. I was so mad, I sat up on the table, I said, "*You* talking about taxes," I said, "if the taxes were added up what my husband and six sons paid in, we'd own this unit."

I said to the nurse, "Get me my clothes, I'm going home." He said, "No, you can't go home." I said, "Yes, I'm going home, you just told me there was nothing wrong with me, I'm going home. Supposing I dies." I got the taxi and came home.

I had to go back again within a week or two, and it was the same doctor there. The nurse told me this doctor was there. I said, "No thank you, I'm not having this doctor." She said, "He's the only doctor on call tonight, you have to see him." He was outside the door and could hear every word I said. I said, "No, I don't want him, I'm not going to have anything to do with him."

After a while a couple of more nurses came in and said this is the only doctor on call so we're going to get him to come in to see you, and that's what they did. I never said "yes" or "no," and then he was the nicest doctor you ever met in your life!

There's a lot of people don't like it . . . In this home we're all kind of strangers

Mrs. Mary Whelan, b. 1902, Conception Bay

I'd be knitting till all hours of the night, socks and mitts. I was only ten years old when I learned how to use knitting needles. But I enjoyed every minute of it.

Here in the home, there's a lot of people don't like it, but I got no fault whatever with this. I can sit here all day knitting, I got my television, my tape recorder, and if I want anything I can go to the kitchen and get it, anything at all. If I get sick in the night, press on my bell. I had a cramp in the stomach the other night, I had heartburn in the beginning, press on my bell and the nurse came in, she went out and brought me in a little drink, cured the heartburn. I have a bottle of liquor. You can bring in your bottle of liquor here.

In this home we're all kind of strangers, we hardly

ever sit down and have a discussion about anything. The only time we get together is for a game of cards, then you're playing cards and you're cussing if you don't win. But in regard to sitting down and having a discussion about anything, we're all strangers. And the woman I share my room with, Oh, my Blessed Lord, she don't talk at all. She's gone since ten o'clock this morning. I'm asleep when she comes back in the night.

The only thing, I had the light on the other night, I was knitting the night of the fireworks, and she called me down to the dirt. She couldn't go to sleep. "Well," I said, "that's all right Mrs. . . . , I'll give up the knitting and let you go to sleep, but I can't sleep with the door open." But I didn't grumble about it, I let her have her way. I pull my curtain right back, because there's an old fellow here that walks up and down the corridor all the time, he don't go to bed. That's why I can't sleep with the door open. We don't talk much, we got nothing in common to talk about.

Everything is changed

Mrs. Joyce Burry, b. 1910, Conception Bay
Everything is changed. One time someone from up here wouldn't be caught going down the shore and marrying somebody; now they're half married from down the shore and up here.

You can't be friendly to a friend anymore

Mr. Fergus Babcock, b. 1911, St. Mary's Bay
You can't be friendly to a friend anymore. You should keep your distance from now on. No, it's bad, it's no good because people don't like you. Now, take a little girl. I used to take babies and wash them and dress them and put powder on them and put napkins on them, but now you can't do that, that's molesting now. You have to let the women do it now and that's it. The world is changed. One bad apple spoils a dozen.

There's two institutions breaking down right now

Mr. Jerome Murphy, b. 1911, Conception Bay
The family was stronger by far than it is today. There's two institutions breaking down right now, and that's the institution of marriage and the institution of the church. Certainly our church, the Catholic church, is breaking down fast. There's a terrible breakdown, what effect it's going to have, I don't know. The institution of marriage, you take now you're involved with sex and the pursuit of sex everywhere, it's a way of life. You can talk all you like about it, but you got to be a realist too and face these things. I've been on the board somewhere where there's religious people telling you what to do and things they didn't have a clue in. They only want you to do things that will land you in hot water anyway.

I'm very concerned about the AIDS

Mr. Billie-Mike Rossiter, b. 1927, Southern Shore
I'm very concerned about the AIDS and what kind of an epidemic it is going to be in the future. Right now I'm concerned because it takes six to seven months to find if a person is carrying HIV. We may be doing it now and not know. And not only that, but for the young people it's frightening and especially with the lifestyle led today.

People have gone away from their religion as far as I'm concerned, too far and living today, it seems that's all the person is worried about. They're not worried about the hereafter, and I think if we were a little more religious minded and listened to the teaching of our church, we wouldn't be faced with an epidemic. Sex-related beliefs are spreading all over.

Alzheimer's, God I hope no one gets that

Mr. Brendan Casey, b. 1922, Bonavista Bay
I'm involved with seniors groups up here in Manuels, so we get together with people my own age on a pretty

regular basis. They are a very healthy group, but we do talk about health problems. You get that all the time. Arthritis mostly, a few heart problems. And just the everyday pain and ache. They talk about "I hope I don't get AIDS." They talk about different things, if someone got arthritis bad. And Alzheimer's, God, I hope no one gets that. I dread to think about it. They say you don't know you have it.

Most of us would be concerned about our memory

Sr. Catherine Daly, b. 1899, Placentia Bay
You see different people with their memory gone. I imagine that's one concern of all of us. We wouldn't like to be like someone else who has no memory, not able to respond, people who were very active in their day.

Of course, as you're getting nearer the end of your pilgrimage, that would be another concern, wondering how you're going to die; in other words, what your death is going to be like.

At this stage of my life I think a lot about cancer, or heart disease

Mr. Cyril Slaney, b. 1926, St. John's
At this stage of my life I think a lot about cancer, or heart disease. Heart disease runs in my mother's family, and my father's family, but I have checkups and they says everything is OK. I got depressed there for a while. I'm on medication for that right now. I hope I soon will be able to give it up because it is awful expensive, drugs. Even though I'm in Blue Cross, it is still very costly. So that is the only thing.

When people my age get together and talk, a lot of them say they are overweight. And the main concerns, they talk about cancer, after you get a certain age that's natural, and heart disease. And there is Alzheimer's now too. That is quite common. We have

a lot of senior citizens in this building and we have
had a few that died from Alzheimer's.

I'm not worried about nothing

I'm not worried about nothing. I'm ready to die
tonight, a heart attack. Let's put it this way, there's
nothing bothers me like that. I can lie down and go to
sleep, unless I got a pain or an ache, I can lie down
and go to sleep and sleep the twenty-four hours,
because my crowd is all settled; my son got his own
business, he's married and got two children and his
wife is a school teacher. My daughter works with the
income tax and she got a knitting machine, she does
her own knitting. The other girls are married and got
their families.

I've got high blood pressure and my angina

Mrs. Phyllis Hawkins, b. 1910, Conception Bay
I've got high blood pressure and my angina. I don't
take too much for that, only the doctor's tablets. I've
had angina since back in '68. I was in hospital for a
while with it, but it's leveled off now pretty well. I take
a tablet every day. It's always up. The last time I was
down the doctor said, "Your blood pressure is good
today. It's normal." I said, "You must be joking, boy."

But thank God it's not too bad now, I manage to get
around and do what I want to do. Bad back, of course,
that goes with old age I suppose. The doctor said it
could be arthritis. But I don't bother the doctors too
much about that. It bothered me yesterday, but I
blame that on the rough road and the van. She takes
the jolts when you're out for a drive.

My two main concerns now are Alzheimer's and the recurrence of cancer

Mrs. Geraldine Reddy, b. 1903, Placentia Bay
My two main concerns now are Alzheimers and the
recurrence of cancer. He had to take away part of my

bowel and he was worried about my liver, afraid he didn't get it all. But he tells me now, five years after, "if there was a recurrence you'd be dead long ago."

Every two months I'm in for a check, with the light down, he's looking around to see what's going on. He's so old now he sits on the stool for his day surgery.

Walking, I think fresh air does you good, and exercise and walk when you can. I walk as much as I can and it's a job to get one of the residents out. I have to go by myself sometimes. One or two I might meet. There are only twenty-three people on this floor and when I was on the first floor, they're mostly sick, but they can walk around. There's not too many in wheelchairs down there, not as many as the second floor. The third floor is the hospital floor. I've never been on it and I wouldn't want to go.

We don't seem to have much in common, a lot of them, there's only a few here on this floor, we got a card club, five of us play cards nearly every night, probably five nights a week. It passes the time away and keeps your brain active, keeps your brain young. That girl that came in here, she's a therapist. We do exercises and one of them plays the piano, and sometimes we dance, waltz around with another woman, and we have sing-a-longs. I don't get any more or any less than the others. And the care here is excellent, whatever you want, they do it.

I don't take any medication; we have a nurse that if I need medication I can get it, but I don't need it. When I came in here after the operation, I was taking a sleeping pill and I couldn't stay awake. I said to the nurse, "I don't need a sleeping pill because I can't stay awake." So I never had one since.

I take a stool softener every day, two a day, morning and night, that looks after my bowels.

Memories, roots and recipes for healthy living

The way many elders look back on the old remedies and health practices is noteworthy. A few informants reject them outright, but most reflect positively on their value, despite being overtaken by "modern" medicines ("I would say the old remedies were good"). Only a few of the vast range of once popular home medicines are still in use and then rarely consistently. Even so, we have a strong sense that the old medicines still provide some informants with feelings of pride in the past, a sense of accomplishment grounded on one's ability to cope. This pride flows from self-sufficiency and independence, especially where the old remedy is still used. Indeed, many of the recipes for healthy living which we also include in this section—and which reiterate points made in chapter 3 on "Looking After One's Health"—explicitly highlight persisting attitudes, values, and in some cases, practices.

I suppose it is foolish, but I believe in it

Mr. James Keilly, b. 1923, St. John's
My remedy for headaches, I suppose it is foolish, but I believe in it. You get vinegar and brown paper and tie it around your head and when the paper got dry, well, dip it down in the vinegar again and tie it around again, and after about a half an hour's time the pain used to go. I don't use it nowadays. I don't have headaches very much. I used to when I was growing up. But I used it once, I think it was last year. I had a real severe headache and it went away.

And I'd take the same when anybody would get a cold now, get a lemon and steep it, and then drink the lemon juice, and take an aspirin and go to bed. We used to use onion and brown sugar, or we had a doctor in Harbour Grace, Dr. Charlie Cron. He was a wonderful doctor. He used to born the babies in our home. We were all born at home.

I keep on using some of the old remedies. For colds, we used to use sometimes goose grease and red flannel to put on your chest. When I get a cold on the chest, I use Minard's Liniment. It takes all the phlegm up off your chest.

Friar's Balsam was another one

Mr. Brendan Casey, b. 1922, Bonavista Bay
I would say that middle-aged people around the bays and the small outports around Newfoundland, I bet they still use the old remedies. We in St. John's don't. But I'm sure there's still people taking Beef Iron Wine. And I'm sure they take cod liver oil, and ginger wine.

Friar's Balsam was another one. You'd take that on a spoon, three or four drops on a spoon for a sore throat. I was somewhere and someone asked me about a certain medicine that we used to sell years ago, and wondered if they could get it now, they went to different drugstores and couldn't find it, Spirits of Nitre. That was for the kidney too.

Old foolishness

Mrs. Alice Harris, b. 1920, St. John's
I'd say mostly older people are still using the old remedies. Now the younger generation are not. My children, they laugh at me when I use Minard's Liniment, stuff like that, for a pain or something is hurting and I rub it in Minard's Liniment. They say, "That's only foolishness, mom." Mostly all the women, I'm over the Mews Centre and we're in the singing, and, say, there's about two hundred people over there that come to sing, and I've been talking to a lot of them, and we all mostly do the same thing. My friend used to tell me the foolishest things. One time I had a toothache real bad and he said, "I'll tell you what to do now. You get a poultice and put it on your elbow and that'll draw the pain right down through your elbow." I don't know if it's belief or what, but the next day, I got up my toothache was better. The

foolish things he would tell you and I would do it. It's the belief I guess, the belief that cured. For a gumboil, they got a raisin and roasted it on top of the stove and put that on the gumboil and that would break it.

A lot of them are ignored now

Mrs. Elizabeth Gibbons, b. 1913, Labrador
It seems like the home remedies, they are all gone down the drain, nobody bothers. A lot of them are ignored now. But if somebody was sick and you couldn't get in to the doctor, older people, you'd go back to some old remedy. In some cases the old remedies, they might be still around.

Most generally now they go to the doctor and get the antibiotics if they got a sore throat or anything like that. Especially since MCP came along and it doesn't cost them anything to go to the doctor, off to the doctor they'll go rather than do something for themselves.

That isn't always good. I had the flu the winter and the doctor came up. I didn't send for him, but somebody told him that I was not well and he came up. He gave me some cough medicine and if I had finished it, I'd be gone down with my man. The first thing, I couldn't eat. I ate a couple of bites of my dinner and I had to go and throw it up. The next thing, I got trouble with my water, I nearly burned up. Then I got constipated, I thought I was going to have to go to the hospital to get rid of it. And the next thing I broke out into an itch and I itched for a month. So I laid the medicine on one side and the next time I went down to get my check up, I got high blood pressure.

I have to go once in a while although I don't go very often, and I told him. I told him, "If I had to finish that medicine that you gave me I wouldn't be coming for any more check ups." He said "Why? What happened?" So I told him, I said, "There must be something in it that I was allergic to." He said, "Yes." He had his pen and he scratched it out on the chart. I said, "I didn't take it and I don't intend to take any more of it." It was a new thing and he was trying it out. He didn't know I was going to be allergic and neither did I. He gave that medicine to somebody else and they had trouble too. I didn't blame him, he thought he was doing a good thing.

I appreciate what medical research has done . . . But

Sr. Teresina Bruce, b. 1902, Codroy Valley
I appreciate what medical research has done and I have used it. I had a couple of operations—tonsillitis and a hysterectomy—and I know there are a lot of things that could have saved people in the olden days that they didn't have and they died for want of it.

But, on the whole, I think they didn't need medicine a lot in those days because the life was healthier. It was an open air life mostly. The food was out of the fields and the sea and the woods. They didn't have the facilities that we have nowadays, but, on the other hand, the need wasn't so great. Perhaps they just about balance out in that way. Although I'm just as glad to live in this present age where you have doctors, dentists, eye specialists and so on. It's certainly a much easier life.

Rest, plenty to eat and no worry

Mrs. Mary Whelan, b. 1902, Conception Bay
The only thing I know is I was born healthy. My mother was a healthy woman. Hard work will never hurt you if you got plenty to eat. Along with the hard work and plenty to eat, you want to get your rest. It's no good for you to be up all night and get out to work tomorrow morning, eight o'clock, you're going to be dead beat when the time comes for you to come off work. You're going to come home too tired to eat. Rest, plenty to eat and no worry. Well, everyone got a bit of worry but not too much. That's my motto.

If people would occupy their minds

Mr. Fergus Babcock, b. 1911, St. Mary's Bay
If people would occupy their minds—sickness is all in the mind, the whole lot of it because when you're doing things, you can't think about anything else. So you forget all about it. Sitting around thinking is the worst thing of all, the worst sickness.

Exercise and a lot of vegetables keep us healthy. Not much good when they're cooked because a lot of vitamins are taken out; eat raw, like eating raw turnips, and raw potatoes, or eating raw cabbage. Eating raw carrots and your eyesight would improve.

I eat the raw cabbage stumps; boy, they're really good, and eating raw carrots and lettuce, I can live on lettuce. I still eats it now. I has cold plates three or four times a week. Tomatoes and I tell you the lettuce, stumpy lettuce, is the best, you know the hard head. Cut it up and get the leaves off, if you can get them off, and the lettuce and the tomatoes and then get the apple and slice your apple up with it. Apples make the flavour.

No junk food, no tin food

Mrs. Phyllis Hawkins, b. 1910, Conception Bay
I never heard tell of people talking about their health, they just went along as they were. I feel everybody was healthy, except regards of a cold or something like that. I think it was that they ate good food. No junk food, no tin food, all this stuff you get from the stores, everything was home grown. When we had this country place, we set our own vegetables and we eat our own vegetables. And cows and hens. And goats and everything, and we eat all our own things. I think, and even people that I know of, they stayed healthy. By eating this food, they stayed healthier. The farmers would come out with their vegetables and you'd buy them, and the meat man would go around to the door and you'd buy the meat off him, you didn't run to the

butcher or the supermarket. So I think that's the reason people were healthier. We need to be like that today.

You had to walk so you kept healthy

Mrs. Alice Harris, b. 1920, St. John's
The mothers were home with their children and the oldest girl would help around with the work and help the other little children. Just ordinary things I suppose. You did your washing on a washing board and tub. People years ago did so much walking that they didn't have to exercise, and they worked too hard. And you walked a lot. Everywhere you went you had to walk, if you didn't have a horse or a carriage. Only rich people had a car. You had to walk and you kept healthy. That's what we had to do.

I don't say anybody got into fitness as such, like today

Mrs. Ronda Peters, b. 1923, Conception Bay
A lot of it was hard work and eat the rough grub, and if you were in good health you were alright. Nobody talked about health then or fitness or anything like that, they just worked hard and that was it. I don't say anybody ever got into fitness as such, like today. Then it was mostly all manual work. A fellow digging a ditch, today he don't even do that, he rents a fellow with a backhoe and he digs the hole, just tells him where to put the shovel.

They did a lot of walking but it was only to work. I don't say they did much walking in the country, not for health reasons. No, they walked because they had to. It was only the street cars in St. John's. I suppose a lot of people really couldn't afford it, even though it was only five cents, but five cents then was a lot.

A lot of people walked who lived up around LeMarchant Road and a little back from there. They all walked. Maybe this is why they're healthy, I don't know.

I take a glass of the honey and apple cider vinegar. You feel it right out to the tips of your fingers

Mrs. Phyllis Hawkins, b. 1923, Conception Bay
Occasionally I take a glass of the honey and apple cider vinegar. It affects your limbs the same as if you took a glass of rum. You feel it right out to the tips of your fingers. It's good. And you won't have it down too long when you'll have to go to the bathroom and pass water. It's really cleansing.

One day at a time, if you're goin' your goin'

Mr. James Keilly, b. 1923, St. John's
To take care of yourself. I do a bit of exercise. Fine days I get out and get the fresh air. I am gone every day when I get a chance. I go on a day like this. I go out in the winter time too. I feels pretty good then.

I don't exactly know, some say I got a cold, some says I am not feeling real good today. We all have our good and bad days. I know I do.

People my age have general complaints. Just complaints that's all. They say my leg is bad today, or I've got a headache or something like that. That's all they say. I takes one day at a time. If you're goin' you're goin.' That's my belief.

Sleep is important for being healthy

Mrs. Mildred Meaney, b. 1923, Placentia Bay
Sleep is important for being healthy. Oh, yes. Although I'm no good to sleep. I'm always used to waking up early in the morning and getting up early. The same thing years ago, when I was growing up. Some people sleep a lot but I was never any good to sleep.

And what you eat is important. You have better food, you have more stuff than you had years ago. More fresh fruit and vegetables. We always had our vegetables but there's more fresh fruit, the right kind of stuff for a diet that you couldn't get years ago.

Worries about the "soft" life

Added to the worries about major changes and uncertainties in present-day society, elders are concerned with liberal lifestyle and the consumerism that has made life today "soft." This softening of modern life prompts questions about their longstanding values, above all self-sufficiency, self-discipline, and hard work. Our remarks in the introduction pointed to bounty and dissolution in Newfoundland history. In the current, increasingly difficult, economic times, many consider that the dissolution of society and a new Depression are inevitable.

Our elders ask for a re-examination of the values of younger generations and the direction of our society. They are particularly concerned about the youth of today, often grandchildren. They see them as much less self-sufficient and self-reliant, less disciplined, less spiritually concerned or guided. They face greater temptations toward sex, eat unhealthy diets and are less inclined to undertake the hard work their parents and grandparents knew. The personal and historical experience of our informants leads them to worry that these attributes may not prepare youth for future uncertainties. How will they make do and survive? It appears that our existing health care system is too costly to maintain as it is. Major changes, including reductions in institutionalized care, are under way. How will the young deal with health and illness? Will they have the mettle and knowledge to survive?

I pity the teenagers

Mrs. Betty Corcoran, b. 1925, Southern Shore
I pity the teenagers today because by advertising those condoms and talking about sex, it's encouraging them to do it, and they know what they are doing and they can use condoms and everything. We must talk about it in the right way, like that police officer on the TV the other day. You shouldn't have sex before you were married. When you hear it on TV, and the way they talk about it, and what you see there

is shocking. There's nude shows and they're topless, oh, my goodness above. Here is where rape comes in again. A girl will go out to the beach, and just a little thing across here and a little thing here, and the man over in the woods probably looking. After all, you know men are sex, a man's desire and what can he do? Thank God my daughters listened to me. I had four daughters and they were married before they ever had children and they tells me about that today. We get into a conversation and say to their children, "Now if a boy touches you or tries to put his hand on your leg, if he don't take it away, give him a smack in the face and he won't bother you anymore."

It's frightening

Mr. David Strong, b. 1917, St. John's
It's frightening. It's terrifying. I do get concerned when I think of my children and grandchildren. That and drugs and the liberal style of young people today. That worries me. I have often said that the Ten Commandments are not necessarily religious. They are a way of life and if we didn't have them, I think that perhaps we'd go to bed every night with a shotgun by our side.

And, of course, the drug part brings out the worst part of sex life

Mr. Warren Brazil, b. 1911, St. John's
Sometimes I think, yes, and sometimes I think no, because I think long ago perhaps the sexual act was not one so much of passion but one more of love and romance. I think the romance part of sex life today has diminished. I think now they say, I imagine a young person meeting a girl, just comes out with two questions, boudoir or cinema? All the romance and the expectations and perhaps the expectations in those days was far greater than the realization. From an educational point of view, I don't think it should be

quite so open as it is, I think it should be at least taught with more reverence than it is today. And, of course, the drug part brings out the worst part of the sex life, I think, people on drugs. You didn't have to contend with that in the old days.

We're living in a different age

We're living in a different age and era. There's more pollution now and there's more social stress. Perhaps one of the other things I was thinking too, now as opposed to then, we weren't lambasted with television to drink more pop, which is absolutely no earthly use to you as far as your health is concerned. If today somebody puts up twenty cents on a bottle of Coke or Pepsi, all hell would break out. Everybody would be writing to the paper, but if bananas were sold for the same price, or milk was sold for the same price, there'd be nothing said about it.

I think people's lifestyle now has to change because of perhaps television. Television has many great aspects, but to lambast a person over the airwaves that they should have a certain kind of pizza pie or certain kind of soft drink and nobody, or very few people are telling you that you should eat more bananas than drink pop, nobody is telling you should have more eggs than chips. Pay eight-five cents for some chips and probably you could get one half to two pounds of bananas for the same price, or pay sixteen cents for one egg and yet go out and put twenty-five cents in for just a little amusement. I think people got to get down to more basics, as far as nutrition is concerned and eat.

The junk foods are killing people today. But in the old days, perhaps food was just as junky when I think about it, salt beef and salt fish could have done as much harm as Pepsi cola does. But we had no choice and there's an awful lot of people that ate salt fish and corned beef and they still lived to be ninety and sometimes one hundred.

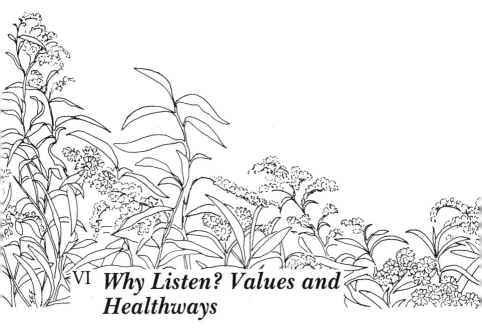

VI *Why Listen? Values and Healthways*

*I*n drawing to a close we focus on the role of values in today's changing society and health care system. We must emphasise that identifying the values of an individual or a community is by no means easy. Social scientists, ethicists, philosophers and others often see values differently; this often relates to their training and whether or not they consider values as interpretations of established behaviour or as guidelines used by individuals for everyday living. Clearly, misunderstandings can arise when people see values with different shades of meaning.

If asked the direct question, "What are your values?" individuals respond in different ways. Most acknowledge a *sense* of values; they know "what I believe in," "what I value in my life." In listening to our informants reveal their values, we heard repeatedly about what they saw as guidelines for everyday living: self-sufficiency ("we really had practically enough to live on without buying anything"); giving one's best effort ("Yes, you had to when there was no doctor or nurse around, you had to work your best"); resourcefulness ("I needed to be resourceful, so you would go to your old home remedies"); pragmatism ("they ate what they could get, whatever was the cheapest"); prudence ("you saved the best way you could"); and a general acceptance of life's rewards and hardships ("you accepted the fact that you lived and you grew old").

Our informants also appreciated and valued a sense of order and self-discipline in various ways ("they wanted you to show your best side and keep up; you had to go to church and that was it; the clergyman told us what to do"). As well, informants revealed a sense of belonging and knowing or accepting one's place in the community ("It was a custom that the men wouldn't go in until the priest would come. The men would gather outside and chat until the priest would come.")

We see here a cluster of individual, interdependent guidelines or values that can be viewed as moral imperatives embedded in everyday living. They promote neither consumer acquisitiveness, nor the open pursuit of status. Moreover, as guidelines for individuals, most were common in a community and accepted as community values.

The values of Newfoundlanders have been considered by other writers, primarily in the 1960s, who were driven by priorities different from our study. Social anthropologists like Melvin Firestone, James Faris, and Louis Chiaramonte, nevertheless, found some similarities with our findings, when they noted an "ethic" of equality, stress on non-conflictual social behaviour, and self-reliance.

The interpretations by others, coupled with the values or guidelines we have identified, point to a basic feature of what we might call a "healthy," a resilient, Newfoundland outport community of the past. Aside from the existence of many common values among individuals in a community, an additional community value is the acceptance of various social mechanisms to control or channel competitiveness, conflict and tensions. Examples include: public deference before authority figures—be they clergy, doctors, elders or merchants; silence and discretion about sexual matters between generations; and the unwritten code of tolerance and cooperation. Also, such calendrical customs and social events as festivals, dancing, drinking, scoffing, gossiping and mummering that helped social integration and to diffuse tensions. Such individual and community values we have identified are rooted in the first half of the twentieth century and earlier, and in particular geographic, social, economic, and religious circumstances of Newfoundland and Labrador. A critical question for those concerned with the future of the province is whether or not those values have survived to the present? We have indicated that our informants are unsure that they persist among their children and grandchildren. Uncertainty is found among others, not just elders, who do not believe that the values of the past survived the radical changes that have occurred in the lives of Newfoundlanders. Such changes include resettlement, universal access to basic medical care, education and a social safety net as a national principle and right. They also include roads, changing technologies, exposure to the mass media, and declining fortunes of the commercial fishery.

If it is accepted that there have been changes in individual and community values, what significance does this have for the future? How can we build a healthy community today—that is, beyond promoting traditional public health policies? One consideration is that the relevance of individual and community values of the past needs to be carefully evaluated. Our informants' feelings that we should return to past values and community structures may not be entirely relevant, especially with the changing roles of many institutions like government and their growing intrusiveness in society. Moreover, we must recognize that, in the changing world we live in, cultural pluralism extends more and more into many small communities. However, we believe strongly that, in developing resilient communities, we must know the past in order to sharpen our questions about the present and the future.

We wish to make one further point in connection with values. We believe that the Newfoundland story challenges our community health care movement, just as it does all physicians, nurses and others in primary health care. It reveals a need to understand past and present values among the elderly, many of whom call upon long-standing guidelines to sustain them through the inconveniences and marginalization of old-age. It is equally important to understand that the values of the younger generations are likely to be substantially different from those of their parents. In suggesting this, we must respond to those who say that everyone who is involved in health care *does* pay attention to values. While this is often true, it is far from clear that sufficient time exists during most interviews or consultations to examine, discover and interpret or gauge the importance of another individual's values, especially those that shape health, illness and recovery.

We comment on such issues because it is too easy to make stereotypic assumptions about people and their communities, and to slide past the individuality and pluralism in our society. It takes time and skill to discover the diversity of values. Perhaps, too, there is a particular difficulty in the area of health care because the "languages" of values, as expressed in official and professional statements, distract us from a close examination of the meanings that patients attach to their values. Does the language of bioethical and legal principles—for example, autonomy, justice, beneficence, and non-maleficence—necessarily reach or appeal to those who stress everyday survival, resourcefulness, prudence and so on? And there is the language of the values enshrined in the Canada Health Act—comprehensiveness, universality, accessibility, portability and public administration. It is easy to talk past each other, especially since much public and academic discussion wrongly suggests that values are uniformly held within communities. Health care practitioners and administrators must appreciate the different languages and understandings about values.

Lastly, we want to comment again on the narratives of which we were a part and have now shared. Stories engage others in a social process that establishes a narrator's individuality, concerns and self-worth. The stories benefit both narrator and audience. They are not merely roles played, such as a doctor's role or a patient's role, but ways to negotiate relationships of mutual understanding, trust and respect.

INFORMANTS

The names of our informants have been changed to give anonymity. The Newfoundland character of names is still reflected in the new ones chosen.

NAME	BORN	COMMUNITY	RELIGION	OCCUPATION
Babcock	Mr Fergus (b.1911)	St. Mary's Bay	RC	brewery worker
Boland	Mr Albert (b.1921)	Southern Shore	RC*	businessman
Brazil	Mr Warren (b.1911)	St. John's	A	watchmaker
Bruce	Sr Teresina (b.1902)	Codroy Valley	RC	teacher
Burry	Mrs Joyce (b.1907)	Conception Bay	RC	governess
Casey	Mr Bredan (b.1922)	Bonavista Bay	RC	park-custodian
Collins	Mrs Julia (b.1921)	Southern Shore	RC	homemaker
Corcoran	Mrs Betty (b.1925)	Biscay Bay	RC	homemaker
Dalton	Mr Kenneth (b.1917)	St. John's	UC	surveyor
Daly	Sr Cathrine (b.1899)	Placentia Bay	RC	teacher
Davis	Mr Abe (b.1913)	Conception Bay	A	trucker/storekeeper
Gibbons	Mrs Elizabeth (b.1913)	Labrador	UC	domestic servant
Gushue	Mrs Viola (b.1930)	St. John's	RC	homemaker
Harris	Mrs Alice (b 1920)	St. John's	UC	homemaker
Hawkins	Mrs Phyllis (b.1910)	Conception Bay	A	secretary
Haynes	Mrs Roberta (b.1921)	Labrador	UC	homemaker
Keilly	Mr James (b.1923)	St. John's	RC	nursing assistant
Meaney	Mrs Mildred (b.1923)	Placentia Bay	RC	foster parent
Murphy	Mr Jerome (b.1911)	Conception Bay	RC	businessman
Myrick	Mrs Sally-Ann (b.1917)	St. John's	A	saleslady
Nolan	Mr Paddy (b.1919)	Southern Shore	RC	fisherman, welder
Peters	Mrs Ronda (b.1923)	Conception Bay	UC	homemaker
Pittman	Mrs Marion (b.1925)	St. John's	RC	saleslady
Reddy	Mrs Geraldine (b.1903)	Placentia Bay	RC	secretary
Rossiter	Mr Billie-Mike (b1927)	Southern Shore	RC	undertaker
Slaney	Mr Cyril (b.1926)	St. John's	RC	lab technician
Strong	Mr David (b.1917)	Ayr, Scotland**	A	administrator
Tarrant	Mr Charles (b.1899)	Southern Shore	RC	fisherman
Whelan	Mrs Mary (b.1902)	Conception Bay	RC	plant worker
Yetman	Mrs Annette (b.1917)	Conception Bay	A	homemaker

* RC = Roman Catholic, A = Anglican, UC = United Church
** Strong was born of Newfoundland parents during WWI in Scotland, and was brought up in St. John's from age two.

GENERAL READING

Healthways relates to numerous areas of study and hopefully adds to them. Like Newfoundland, however, our study remains distinct. We believe the best way to illustrate the affinities with other works is through a brief bibliographical essay. The studies mentioned below will introduce readers to relevant themes and provide further information on topics covered in or related to our narratives. While the time frame of our narratives is the first half of this century, many of the works cited are often of a later date. However, they generally make retrospective comparisons between earlier contemporary lifestyles and other ways of life.

Our introduction emphasizes the importance of listening to people's stories as a way of understanding their life's values. We acknowledge one particular book that focused us: Eva J. Salber's <u>Don't Send Me Flowers When I'm Dead. Voices of Rural Elderly</u>, Durham: Duke University Press, 1983. Salber gives us a minimum of interpretation of the moving narratives she offers. In some respects the struggles she reveals in the lives of North Carolina rural people bear comparison with those faced by Newfoundlanders of more or less the same generation.

Since the early 1980s, researchers from many disciplines have shown interest in narratives. To query the whole approach of the narrative as a valid technique for discovering patterns and attitudes in peoples' lives, especially as they look back over time, we offer additional readings. D. Boden and D. Biebly, *The past as resource: a conversational analysis of elderly talk*, <u>Human Development</u>, 26: 308-19, 1983, emphasizes the importance of a relaxed, informal atmosphere and conversational style interview to enhance the fullness of the data. L. Brown, *et al*, <u>A Guide to Reading Narratives of Conflict and Choice for Self and Relational Voices</u>, (Monograph No. 1) Cambridge, MA: Harvard Graduate School of Education, Center for the Study of Gender, Education, and Human Development, 1988, offers a more detailed understanding of interpreting interview data. They identify points for discerning between a contextual believability and obvious glorification. Also worthy of note is E.M. Bruner who explores interviewing techniques in *Ethnography as narrative*. In V.W. Turner and E.M. Bruner (Eds.), The Anthropology of Experience, Urbana, IL: University of Chicago Press, 1986. Interpretation of narratives is discussed in W. Martin, Recent Theories of Narrative, Ithaca, NY: Cornell University Press, 1986. J. Bruner examines reliability in the narrative in his *The narrative construction of reality*, Critical Inquiry, 18: 1-21, 1991. A further useful reference is Susan E. Chase, *Taking narrative seriously: Consequences for method and theory in interview studies,* in Ruthellen Josselson and Amia Liebich (Eds.), Interpreting Experience: The Narrative Study of Lives, V3, Newbury Park, CA: Sage, 1995. She argues that all forms of narratives share fundamental concerns with making sense of experience.

An annual periodical edited by R. Josselson and A. Lieblich, The Narrative Study of Lives, Newbury Park, CA: Sage, discusses the narrative approach and its methodological issues. Three volumes are currently in print: volume 1 (1993) presents a general overview of the narrative method; volume 2 (1994) focuses on exploring identity and gender; and volume 3 (1995) narrows in on interpreting experience. A more recent comprehensive discussion of the narrative is found in J. A. Holstein and J. F. Gubrium, The Active Interview, Thousand Oaks, CA: Sage, 1995. They stress that eliciting data is an interactive process; it forces a stronger focus and prevents informants from going off on a "tangent." We caution, however, that what the interviewer may view as tangential may be more important to the respondent than the interviewer's directed question. This raises the basic issue: *Whose priorities are most important in the narrative exchange?*

To address the issue of priorities, an excellent illustration is found in patients' telling their stories to health caregivers. These patients regard life story telling as therapeutic, for example to deal with unresolved conflicts. However, overemphasis on therapeutics risks appropriating storyteller autonomy, and converting their stories into commodities, distortion, and suppression of individual and cultural uniqueness. Such arrogation of patient autonomy fits the tendency in biomedical institutions "to infantilize people who are physically debilitated," and should be recognized. See L.J. Price, *Life stories of the terminally ill: Therapeutic and anthropological paradigms*, <u>Human Organization</u>, 54(4): 462-9, 1995. Various studies raise the issue of therapeutic benefits (helping, coping, self-esteem and so on) to be had from giving reminiscences. Among them are: L. Pearlin, and C. Schooler, *The structure of coping*, <u>Journal of Health and Social Behavior</u>, 19: 2-2, 1978; P. Brickman, *et al, Models of helping and coping*, <u>American Psychologist</u>, 37(4): 368-84, 1992, and V. B. Newbern, *Sharing the memories: The value of reminiscence as a research tool*, <u>Journal of Gerontology Nursing</u>, 18(5): 13-8, 1992. Another example is B.L. Roberts, R. Dunkle, M. Hano, *Physical, psychological and social resources as moderators of the relationship of stress to mental health of the very old*, <u>Journal of Gerontology</u>, 49(1): 35-43, 1994. No matter how the interviewer's role is conceived, the relationship is always interactive. Information elicited is always subject to the purpose and pose of the parties in the exchange.

Our interest in listening and talking to elders focused us on aging and its complexities, ranging from general issues of communication to more technical language problems. The broader contexts of communication and aging are discussed in: Carl W. Carmichael, *Communication and gerontology: Interfacing disciplines*, <u>Western Speech Communication</u>, Spring: 121-129, 1976, and J. F. Nussbaum, T. Thompson, and J. D. Robinson, <u>Communication and Aging</u>, New York: Harper, 1988. The narrower features of language are noted in E. B. Ryan, *et al, Psycholinguistic and social psychology components of communication by and with elderly*, <u>Language and Communication</u>, 6: 1-24, 1986; Susan Kemper and Cheryl Anagnopoulos, *Language and aging*, <u>Annual Review of Applied Linguistics</u>, 10: 37-50, 1989. Intergenerational talk is covered in E. B. Ryan and D. G. Johnston, *The influence of communicative effectiveness on evaluations of younger and older speakers*, <u>Journal of Gerontology</u>, 42: 163-6: 1987 and E. B.

Ryan, *Intergenerational talk to elders - Is there bias?*, Gerontological Forum '91, Lakehead University: Thunder Bay, 1991. Identity factors are found in Nikolas Coupland, *et al*, *Elderly self-disclosure: interactional and intergroup issues*, Language and Communication, 8(2): 109-133, 1988, and Nikolas Coupland, *et al*, *Formulating Age: Dimensions of age identity in elder talk*, Discourse Processes, 14: 87-106, 1991. Communication issues regarding health are found in Howard Giles, Nikolas Coupland, and John Weiman (Eds.), Communication, Health, and the Elderly, Manchester: Manchester University Press, 1990.

In chapter one we indicate that examination of our interview data led us to identify a congeries of unprioritized attitudes and expectations (self-sufficiency, a sense of community etc.). We refer to them as "values" that our informants remember as important to their lives and health when growing up. They serve to anchor, distinguish and arm them even now in their retirement. We admit, however, that it is not easy to impute values to a people's behavior; after all, they are abstractions from highly complex, dynamic and situational social and cultural behavior. Current critical social science perspectives on the many issues (e.g., generation, measurement, transmission, constancy, function) raised about values can be found in an overview essay by Michael Hechter, *Values research in the social and behavioural sciences*, in Michael Hechter, Lynn Nadel, and Richard E. Michod (Eds.), The Origin of Values, New York: Aldine De Gruyter, 1993, pp1-24. Also from the same volume is Fredrik Barth, *Are values real?*, pp31-46. A second useful volume of value is Colin Fraser (Ed.), The Social Psychological Study of Widespread Beliefs, Oxford: Claredon Press, 1990.

Geographers have extensively documented the European settlement of Newfoundland. See especially: W. Gordon Handcock, So Longe as There Comes Noe Women: Origins of English Settlement in Newfoundland, St. John's: Breakwater Books, 1989; and John J. Mannion's Irish Settlements in Eastern Canada, Toronto, University of Toronto Press, 1974, and Point Lance in Transition, Toronto, McClelland and Stewart Ltd., 1975.

Values identified in our narratives are seen in whole or part in other studies. Newfoundland and Labrador communities have received much attention from social anthropologists and sociologists since the 1960s. It may be the most thoroughly studied area of Canada in social science terms, but the literature has its limitations. The social anthropological literature, in particular, is based upon intensive studies of a small number of outports in distant and distinct areas of the province. Its outcomes are mixed in consequence of different authors, concerns and approaches. Although not easy to compare, one can find common threads among these studies. James Faris, Cat Harbour: A Newfoundland Fishing Settlement, ISER (see endnote), 1966, describes elements of the "moral order" and its "behavioral prescriptions" in an inshore fishing outport on Newfoundland's east coast. Tom Philbrook, Fishermen, Logger, Merchant, Miner: Social Change and Industrialism in Three Newfoundland Communities, ISER, 1966, compares three different communities that illustrate a shift to industrialization and a cash economy, now termed "market place values." John Szwed, Private Cultures and Public Imagery: Interpersonal Relations in a Newfoundland Peasant Society, ISER, 1966, with a strongly functionalist bent, describes life in a fishing and farming community of the Codroy Valley. Melvin Firestone, Brothers and Rivals: Patrilocality in Savage Cove, ISER, 1967, focuses on life in Savage Cove, a "folk community" on the Northern Peninsula. In respect to its social structure and its "egalitarian ethic," it is the lynchpin for much of the social interaction in this context, and the restraint of competition and conflict. Lastly, Louis Chiaramonte, Craftsmen and Client Contracts: Interpersonal Relations in a Newfoundland Fishing Community, ISER, 1970, presents an account of life in Harbour Deep, a south coast fishing community. This study contrasts with that of Savage Cove in its more diverse fisheries adjustment and what seems a greater range of productive alternatives at least for men. Greater emphasis is placed on individual self-reliance than on cooperation and community. An egalitarian ethic, however, remains important in their social relationships. A further useful source is Tom Nemec's unpublished Ph.D. dissertation, *An ethno-historical and ethnographic study of the cod fishery at St. Shotts, Newfoundland*, Ann Arbor, Michigan: University of Michigan, 1980. Nemec describes life in an Irish Catholic inshore fishing community in the area from which some of our informants come.

Despite the ethic of equality, stress on non-conflictual social behavior, and sufficiency and self-reliance evident in these studies from the 1960s, the divisive issue of class and power runs through much of the same literature cited. It records what seems an old and often exploitative credit or truck relationship between fishers and merchants in a largely cashless economy. Exploring the nature of this relationship and its implications for Newfoundland society and culture has been and remains an important concern among historians, social anthropologists and other scholars. This issue is well addressed in Gerald M. Sider, Culture and Class in Anthropology and History, Cambridge: Cambridge University Press, 1986, and Jerry Bannister's recent overview essay, *A species of vassalage: The issue of class in the writing of Newfoundland history*, Acadiensis, 24(1): 133-44, 1995. See also Nemec's discussion of the priest's role ("They were above everyone else and had no equals save other clergy.") in the Irish Catholic inshore fishing outport of St. Shotts. Here "communal egalitarianism" prevailed in ordinary relationships (op cit, pp193-200).

We must also note: G. L. Pocius, A Place to Belong. Community Order and Everyday Space in Calvert, Newfoundland, Montreal: McGill-Queen's University Press, 1991, and J. T. Omohundro, Rough Food: The Seasons of Subsistence in Northern Newfoundland, ISER, 1994. A worthwhile early collection of essays about Newfoundland, its people, culture and development is found in The Book of Newfoundland, V1-6, J. R. Smallwood (Ed.), St. John's: Newfoundland Book Publishers, (various dates); also the more recent Encyclopedia of Newfoundland, St. John's: Newfoundland Book Publishers (various editors and dates. Many essays are by Newfoundlanders themselves. Recounting first hand experiences of growing up in the Newfoundland outport during the first part of this century, for example, Isabel Scott's *The Fisherman's Wife*, V1. For fine examples of words, reflecting local usage and dialect coloring, especially describing traditional home remedies, see G. M. Story, W. J. Kirwin and J. D. A. Widdowson (Eds.) Dictionary of Newfoundland English, (2nd ed.) Toronto: University of Toronto Press, 1990.

An excellent view of the flesh and tenor of interaction in Newfoundland's small communities is presented by contributors to the essay collection Christmas Mumming in Newfoundland, Herbert Halpert and George Story (Eds.), Toronto: University of Toronto Press, 1969. For example, in his essay, *Mumming in an outport fishing settlement*, pp128-44, anthropologist James Faris illustrates the restrained nature of social life in outport communities:

> There is in Cat Harbour a strict avoidance of physical conflict, of overheated arguments, and of overt emotional expression in general . . . Conflict and hostility must be avoided or at least repressed in so small and isolated a community where the social networks are so totally intertwined. p139.

This is not to say that Newfoundlanders lived in social "straitjackets." There were many occasions for creative and controlled departure from this restrained sociality, as in Christmas mumming, a custom with centuries long European roots.

Focusing more on biographical material, we have: V. Butler, Supposin I Dies In D'Dory, St. John's: Jespersen, 1977; H. C. Murray, *More than Fifty Percent. Women's Life in a Newfoundland Outport 1900-1950*, St. John's: Breakwater, 1979; W. W. Wareham (Ed.), The Little Nord Easter: Reminiscence of a Placentia Bayman, St. John's: Breakwater, 1980; and, J. B. Mifflen's *Journey to Yesterday in the Out-harbours of Newfoundland*, St. John's: Cuff Publications, 1983.

By 1965, sixteen years after Confederation with Canada, a resettlement program was introduced by the Newfoundland and federal governments. It was an effort to bring a 20th century living standard and its ways to hundreds of small scattered outports. This displaced an ongoing, largely voluntary process of internal migration. The government's "resettlement program," however, became a watershed of sorts between "traditional" outport lifestyles and culture, and those of a more industrial way of life. Studies of the resettlement program record the experiences of those who resettled and those who resisted. The consequences of what was often found to be forced internal migration provide us with interesting insights. Noel Iverson and D. Ralph Matthews, <u>Communities in Decline: An Examination of Household Resettlement</u>, St. John's: ISER, 1968, is a survey-based study of several communities that moved; Ralph Matthews, <u>There's No Better Place Than Here</u>, Toronto: Peter Martin Associates, Ltd., 1976, investigated several communities whose residents chose not to move. For a regional, ethno-historical perspective on southern Labrador communities see John Kennedy, <u>People of the Bay and Headland</u>, Toronto: University of Toronto Press, 1995. And see John Kennedy, <u>Labrador Village</u>, Prospect Heights, Ill.: Waveland Press, 1996, for a view of a contemporary coastal outport.

Most of the social anthropological literature of the 1960s about Newfoundland and Labrador community life was male-authored. It is no surprise that women's roles receive little attention and they are sometimes misinterpreted. Subsequent anthropological, historical and sociological literature gradually overcame this androcentric bias. It has built a more balanced and realistic understanding of women, gender roles and experience in these communities and the important theoretical issues they raise.

Strong female voices are heard in the 1970s. For example, the life of women and their families in Labrador communities during much of the first half of this century is well illustrated by Elizabeth Goudie's biography, <u>Women of Labrador</u>, Toronto: Peter Martin Associates, 1973. Her story reveals as her writing collaborator, David Zimmerly, says in his introduction, "the freedom, the independence, and the self-sufficiency of the Labrador people." Goudie grew on the

Labrador, became a trapper's wife and witnessed the gradual decline and loss of small communities with the shift of population to growing centers. We have already mentioned H. C. Murray, <u>More Than Fifty Percent: Women's Life in a Newfoundland Outport 1900-1950</u>, St. John's, Breakwater, 1979, and there are others from this decade.

During the 1980s to the present there has been a veritable explosion of insightful discourse about women's roles and their related theoretical issues. For example, there are: M. Govanninni's monograph, <u>Outport Nurse</u>, MUN:Medicine, 1988; Dona L. Davis, <u>Blood and Nerves: An Ethnographic Focus on Menopause</u>, ISER, 1988. This latter work is probably the first important medical anthropological study on Newfoundland women's lives. Based upon fieldwork in a southwest coast outport, her findings on lifestyles, gender roles, and values support the perspectives expressed in this present volume. See also Dana L. Davis, *Blood and Nerves Revisited:* <u>Medical Anthropology Quarterly</u> (1997) Vol. 11(1): 3-20. An interesting contrastive account of women in a variety of fishing societies is found in Jane Nadel-Klein and Dona L. Davis, (Eds.), <u>To Work and To Weep</u>, ISER, 1988. Further volumes on women are: J. McNaughton's Ph.D. thesis, *The Role of the Newfoundland Midwife in Traditional Health Care 1900-1970*, MUN:Medicine, 1989; Cecilia Benoit, <u>Midwives in Passage</u>, ISER, 1991, and R.M. Piercey, <u>True Tales of Rhoda Maude: Memoirs of an Outport Midwife</u> (J. McNaughton, Ed.), Faculty of Medicine, Memorial University of Newfoundland, 1992.

The most recent appreciation of women in Newfoundland society include: Marilyn Porter, <u>Place and Persistence in the Lives of Newfoundland Women</u>, Aldershot, England: Avebury, 1993; Linda Kealey (Ed.), <u>Pursuing Equality: Historical Perspectives on Women in Newfoundland and Labrador</u>, ISER, 1993; and Carmelita McGrath, Barbara Neis, and Marilyn Porter (Eds.), <u>Their Lives and Times: Women in Newfoundland and Labrador</u>, St. John's: Killick Press, 1995.

Regarding sexuality and fertility, our informants recall what seems a strong sense of shame around open discussion and display between generations. Little of what took place about sexuality among peers is revealed, and nothing about how these subjects were treated in other kinds of discourse, e.g. humour, songs, and story telling. However, the "silence" described may be usefully compared with descriptions of life in North Atlantic Christian fishing communities. In particular, some Portuguese fishing communities are thought to have more open and "archaic" (yet also somewhat "modern") forms of reference to sexual matters. See Jan Brogger, <u>Nazare: Women and Men in a Prebureaucratic Portuguese Fishing Village</u>, New York: Harcourt, Brace Jovanovich, 1992; and for a rare serious examination of how gender is socially constructed in the fishing village, see Sally Cole, <u>Women of the Praia: Work and Lives in a Portuguese Coastal Community</u>, Princeton, New Jersey: Princeton University Press, 1991.

For a list of writings on medicine and health see Isabel Hunter and Shelagh Wotherspoon, <u>A Bibliography of Health Care in Newfoundland</u>, MUN:Medicine, a 1986. The role of the outport nurse is described in Joyce Nevitt, <u>Whitecaps and Blackbands: Nursing in Newfoundland to 1934</u>, St. John's: Jesperson, 1978. A useful biographical survey on medical service along the Newfoundland coast includes: P. Troake, <u>No One Is a Stranger. Reminiscences on Tuberculosis, Traditional Medicine, and Other Matters</u>, MUN:Medicine, 1988; G. Saunders, <u>Dr. John Olds</u>, Breakwater: St. John's, NF, 1994; and R. Rompkey's, <u>Grenfell of Labrador: a biography</u>, Toronto: University of Toronto Press, 1992.

Sources on dental health in Newfoundland and Labrador include historical overviews written by dentists. In particular, E.P. Kavanagh's offers short accounts in *History of dentistry in Newfoundland*, <u>Journal of Canadian Dental Association</u>, 18(6): 354, 1952 and *Progress in dentistry*, In <u>The Book of Newfoundland</u> V6, J.R. Smallwood (Ed.), St. John's: Newfoundland Book Publishers, 414-5, 1975.

Paul S. Dinham discusses how outport Newfoundlanders view and react to mental illness in his volume, <u>You Never Know What They Might Do: Mental Illness in Outport Newfoundland</u>, St. John's: ISER, 1977. Dinham's work is a strong caution against making facile interpretations of differences between rural and urban mental illness hospital admission rates. For example, in the investigated outport fishing communities, Dinham found greater "toleration of abnormal behavior and dealing with it within the community . . . [that] lowers the need for consultation with professionals (p47)." For the more severe mentally ill, however, this meant a higher proportion being admitted to hospital from those areas than from urban areas. The history of mental illness medical treatment in Newfoundland is examined in Patricia Smith O'Brien, <u>Out of Mind, Out of Sight: A History of the Waterford Hospital</u>, St. John's: Breakwater, 1989. J.K. Crellin presents a comprehensive overview of traditional health care in <u>Home Medicine: The Newfoundland Experience</u>, Montreal: McGill-Queens, 1994.

Note: Acronym **ISER** refers to Institute for Social and Economic Research, Memorial University of Newfoundland, St. John's, NF.

INDEX

Abernathy, Nurse (southern shore), 127
abortion, 37, 80, 81, 83-84, 90
accidents, 28, 56; cot, 127; fixing fingers, 42-43
adoption, 53, 77; informal, 53, 81, 86
Angela, Sister (St. John's), 104
Anglican(s), 119; Church Lads' Brigade, 59
babies, beliefs: around the bay, 84; doctor brought it to me, 88-89; feeding bottles, 87
Barry, Mrs. (Fermeuse), 20
Bauline South, 115
Bay Bulls, 46, 114, 119, 129
bedwarming, heated rocks, 30
beliefs (see also food): activity, 150; blessing, 123; contagion, 103; chills, 99; disease, 91-92; early rising, 152; fairies, 110; fresh air, 102, 103; full moon, 115; ghosts, 112; hard work, 151; good eyesight, 150; junk food, 150-151; old hag, 92; sharing food, 99; sleep, 152; smoking, 138; tack, 97; tuberculosis, 94, 103; warm feet, 138; wet feet, 99-100
Bell Island, 29, 31
belonging, sense of, 9
Bennett, Nurse (Labrador), 105
Black, J. R., 59
bleeding, 104-106, 119; stopping: ice, 105; charmer, prayer, 119; "stopper," 27; scapular, 126
Blue Cross, 143
Bonavista Bay, 5
bone-setter, 122
Boston, 52
Bouden, Mrs. (southern shore), 124
Bowrings, 23
Bristol's Cove, 19
Calvert, 96
Canada Health Act, 160
Canning, Mrs. (southern shore), 125
Capahayden, 126
Cape Broyle, 109, 114
Cape St. Mary's, 23
Carbonear, 5
Cartwright, 41, 45
Cashin, Martin, Dr. 51
Catholic, 104: church, 142; communities, 13; Mass, 110; relics, 25; sacraments, 22; southern shore, 12
Chafe, Philomena, Mrs. (St. John's), 104

charms, 27; charmers, 120-121
childbirth: at home, 146; breech, 110; complications, 111, 130
children, 15: chores, 14; death, 18, 29, 32, 102; discipline, 36, 44; games, 20, 35, 40, 41; guns, 45; roles, 32
Christmas, 13, 30, 65, 110
church: planning families, 78; shaped individual lives, 13; spiritual and social centre, 12
class distinction, 16
clothes: clean, 58; dry, 106; scald, 100
Codroy Valley, 5, 65
Coles, Robert, 1
communities: change, 13, 75, 141-142; cultural pluralism, 159; egalitarian, 16; health care movement, 161; healthy, 12, 72, 159; life, 4; maritime, 4; neighbourly, 73-74; outport, 10; power structure, 9; Protestant, 13; resources, 58; spirit, 21; support, 12-13, 14, 35, 68, 72, 115, 117, 122, 124
Conception Bay, 5
contraception, 77
cooking, 21
coping, 3, 157-160; inner strength, 93; worry, 144
Cowan, Jack (St. John's), 33
cream, scald, 31
Cron, Charlie, Dr. 146
Daniel's Harbour, 45
Dawe, Lewis (Labrador), 105
death, attitudes, 143
dental care, 58, 60, 105-106, 147-148: gumboil, 148; home remedy, 147, 148
Depression, the, 29, 47, 51, 54, 137
Devereux, Jim (Conception Bay), 122
diet, quality, 67
disabilities (see also illness): mental, 111, 113, 115; physical, 109-110, 111, 112
diseases (see illness)
doctors, 28, 129: attitudes to, 128, 139-140; authority, 128; calling, 130; childbirth, 124; competency, 127, 131; ease of access, 130, 139; faith in, 131; payment, 130; turnover, 117
dole, 30, 111
domestic service (in-service), 33, 34, 41, 49, 74, 122
driving license, elderly fitness, 37-38